WHEN

GOD

BECOMES

BRIAN JOHNSON

REAL

THANK YOU

* * *

Jenn. I love you, babe. Your strength, passion and heart for God amaze me. You never let go of His faithfulness or promises for both of us. You saw the vision and ran with me every step of the way.

Haley, Téa, Braden and Ryder. You are the gifts in my life that still overwhelm me each and every day. You keep my heart grounded and are my constant joy. Your mom and I pray for you daily and are so excited to see you walk in all that God has for you.

Mom and Dad. From the first moment this season started at just seven years old, your steadfast belief in the goodness of God anchored me and allowed me to know that I would find freedom. Circumstances never changed your belief. Your unwavering commitment to this truth has changed the lives of countless people. Your perseverance, humility and relentless pursuit of God inspire me every day.

Joel Taylor. You've always had my back. You heard the dreams in our hearts and made them come to life. You shouldered more than I can say, and I know that we would not be where we are without you.

Jason Borneman. You brought so much fun into our lives and laughter into our house. You had such a clear understanding of my journey and brought peace when I needed it most. You are the definition of a true friend.

Holly Brunson. We both know that this book wouldn't have been completed if you hadn't encouraged me to keep searching for the right words and have the courage to tell my story. Only you and I will know the countless hours and edits and re-edits we went through. You helped me find words for my story when I would have given up. Thank you for helping bring my story to life. You went and found the puzzle pieces and then brought it all back together.

Kris and Kathy Vallotton. You went before me into a hard place and had the courage to come out on the other side. Thank you for the crucial moments of bringing me hope and being my strength in that season when I didn't have it.

Seth Haines. Thank you for your help in bringing this book to life! Your insight and help were invaluable.

Bethel Music Community. You're the promise of so many of the prophetic words Jenn and I've been given over the past twenty-five years. Your personal commitment and faithfulness to God inspire and move me. What a team God has given us. I'm more than proud of your passion and work to let the world experience and encounter God.

ENDORSEMENTS

* * *

We live in a world that works so hard to make everything appear just right. This is especially true within the church, where if you are a leader, you have such a high expectancy to never show or have weakness. My friend Brian Johnson shatters all these facades to pieces with his book When God Becomes Real. *Brian helps us see once again the power and lifeline of praise, not just on the mountain peak, but deep in the valley. I know you will find strength, hope and encouragement for your own journey through this book.*

CHRIS TOMLIN

I am sure that most of us who have picked up this book have had specific moments and events in our lives when God becomes real. Brian's story told throughout these pages is such a beautiful depiction of God's love, power and faithfulness in seasons where He really is the only option to turn to. This book is uplifting, insightful and passes along courage to keep believing and going through those moments of our lives one step at a time. I believe the words and tools in these pages are going to help every person who reads them in a profound way. There are deeper levels of freedom and relationship Jesus wants to take us to and this book is going to help you get there.

KARI JOBE

When God Becomes Real *is Brian's incredible testimony of making what God has done for him bigger than what any person or life experience did to him. This book will challenge you to cultivate a life of worship and immerse yourself in Scripture so that you too can develop a faith that cannot be shaken, no matter what you may face.*

CHRISTINE CAINE,
BEST-SELLING AUTHOR, FOUNDER A21 AND PROPEL WOMEN

I am so grateful that my friend Brian Johnson has put into a book his story in such a profoundly vulnerable and honest way. I've often said that the greatest weapon I know against the darkness of this world is the worship of the one who has overcome it. Brian learned this early on in life not as some sort of head knowledge he picked up in church but truly as heart knowledge he learned from his father out of a desperate need for its truth. It's no mystery to me why God has chosen Brian to birth a worship movement that has traveled the earth.

JASON INGRAM

There are moments in life when the enemy simply comes in like a flood...and in those seasons it feels like drowning would almost be sweet relief compared to the terror that ensues. In When God Becomes Real *Brian Johnson opens his heart and bares his soul as he shares his most personal and powerful life story. I am confident that this book will lead your heart to the welcome truth of God's Presence in the midst of any trying time...declaring again the wonder and power of Christ Jesus, the name that is above every other name.*

DARLENE ZSCHECH

To sit across from Brian and hear firsthand the story of his chronic struggle with anxiety is to take a tumble down the rabbit hole into a Mad Hatter's tea party where perception and reality are opposing forces. Who would have believed that such a gifted worship leader and consummate outdoorsman had spent so much of his very young life in a world of chaos. Brian's journey into the heart of God's freedom is a lifeline for so many others struggling in secret and self-imposed shame, desperate to find their way back to the surface.

MATT CROUCH

CEO OF TBN

Something happens when we own our stories, when we tell the truth from the secret to the stage. There is a vulnerability and an authority that can only come when I share how Jesus rescued me. We each have a story to tell, and no one can tell it for us. If there is anything I have learned about Brian after running with him and serving him these last ten years, it is this: he is true. He is unapologetically himself, and his tenderness and honesty will be a catalyst for change in your life, just as it has been in our community.

STEFFANY GRETZINGER

We were born into a war. All of us. And regardless of the circumstances surrounding each child's upbringing, no one escapes this reality. The battle ground for this war is the mind. The enemy of our souls tries to influence our thoughts and values because he fears our relationship with and our ability to represent our perfect Father. We were made in the image of God, who created all things. The world is crying out for an accurate creative expression that comes from those who have heartfelt understanding of being made in His image. But if we yield to fear, anxiety, self-criticism, and the like, our effectiveness is seriously compromised.

Our son Brian gives us a glimpse into his journey out of fear, panic, and anxiety in this raw but wonderful book, When God Becomes Real. *It is honest, redemptive and filled with insights to help readers taste greater victory for themselves. The struggle is real. But the victory is even more real—a much greater reality. This book will give hope to countless people feeling all alone as they face a battle in their mind, some thinking they are going crazy.* When God Becomes Real *will also help friends and family members gain insights on how to love, help and support those going through their dark night of the soul. Read it, and watch how God equips you for victory, both for yourself and those under your influence.*

BILL & BENI JOHNSON

THE PRIVILEGED PARENTS OF ERIC, BRIAN AND LEAH

BETHEL CHURCH, REDDING, CA

CONTENTS

FOREWORD

* * *

Brian Johnson is no ordinary pastor's kid. In all my years of traveling, I've met a lot of pastors' kids, but few like Brian. As the pioneer of Bethel Music, Brian has led countless individuals into unparalleled depths of worship. However, what I admire the most about Brian is his relentless pursuit of God that is driven by a deep conviction that God is real. Despite all his accomplishments, he refuses to become complacent.

For this reason, I am thankful Brian has written *When God Becomes Real*. His life is consistent with the message of this book. Brian candidly shares his journey of discovering God through personal experience. He challenges us to confront the very thing many spend most of their lives avoiding—pain! Brian offers a unique perspective toward pain, sharing that our darkest moments can become defining moments, moments in which God becomes real! Often, in times of difficulty, what we truly believe is tested. It's in these moments when we learn to use worship as both a weapon and a lifeline. As we do, we'll be assured that God is good, even when life is not. When we finally face our pain head-on, we are positioned to be propelled further into our destinies. As mentioned within the book, Brian leaned into this truth: worship is more than singing songs to God; it's investing in our relationship with Him, even when we don't feel like it or when circumstances are difficult.

I highly recommend reading *When God Becomes Real*. You'll receive the encouragement to press on until, like Job, you can confess, "I admit I once lived by rumors of you; now I have it all firsthand—from my own eyes and ears!" (Job 42:5).

A personal encounter with God awaits you!

John Bevere
Author/Minister
Messenger International

INTRODUCTION

* * *

In so many ways, I've had the best life. I was born into a family that most people would dream of. My parents love God and are the most humble, kind and supportive people I've ever known. As a child, my mom gave me some of my earliest memories of being with God, and there wasn't anything I couldn't share with her after a hard day at school. Whenever my brother, sister or I needed them, they were fully present. They never gave me a reason to question their unconditional love or the unconditional love and goodness of God. And if this book was a collection of stories about the good times we had, it'd take thousands of pages to tell them all.

And then there's my incredible wife, Jenn. She's been my partner in every way, and she's stuck with me through thick and thin (as you'll see in this book). She's led worship with me from almost the first moment we were together. She's written songs that have changed my life and the lives of so many others. She's given me the gift of four amazing kids, and if this story were about our marriage, it'd be mostly happy.

Jenn and I built Bethel Music with one of my best friends, Joel Taylor. He often put words to our dreams and has always had my back. I have a dream job helping to lead Bethel Music, creating music with friends from around the world, and preaching at schools and conferences. I'm surrounded by some of the best leaders and musicians who have pushed me to be the best I can be.

We have an amazing community and church. Bethel has been a healing place for people all over the world. It's the place where it all started for Jenn and me. There are so many memories in that sanctuary of God moving and witnessing encounters where people were changed forever. My life has been changed forever. I'm forever grateful for our church and local community.

When I look at my life, it's been a gift. I could go on and on about the blessings and joys of my life. But even the most joyful lives have their share of hard times. I'm no exception.

This book doesn't tell the full and balanced story of my life. It doesn't share all the wonderful things that happened along the way. Instead, this book is about the two major battles—one I fought as an adult, and one I fought as a child. The circumstances behind each of these battles were quite different, but both threw me into a darker season of life, a season where I had no other option but to trust God. And as you follow me through my journey and ultimately into victory, you'll see just how I discovered the goodness of God.

I wrote this book so that you could understand the circumstances that led me through two great battles, and how I came out on the other side. I don't highlight all the joys and victories in my life because those stories won't show you how I entered the dark night of my soul and how I found the light again. And as you read this book, I hope you'll find yourself, your family and your friends in the pages. I hope you'll see how God wants to rescue you from your own panic, anxiety, fear and doubt. More than anything though, I hope you'll experience this truth: everything changes when God becomes real.

ONE

CATCHING LIZARDS

* * *

This is how it started: some invisible hand reached in, grabbed my lungs, and squeezed; the pressure settled across my chest, then my shoulders. My hands began to shake; the air thinned; my fear thickened. I raised my arms over my head, locked my fingers and tried to catch my breath.

What is this?

I looked at the river, then looked around the area until I laid eyes on him. There was my son Braden turning over rocks and looking under logs. He was lizard hunting, just like my brother, Eric, and I did when we were his age. Eyes squinting in the sun, mud splotches up to his shins, he was having the time of his life and had no idea that some invisible force was creeping up on me. Something was very wrong.

Braden's hand shot under a log, and he pulled out a lizard. He turned and held his fist in the air, yelling, "I got him, Dad!" I did my best to smile back and wave, but the invisible walls were already closing in, even in the wide-open spaces by the river. I took a deep breath, tried to hold those walls back, and that was when the surge of adrenaline rushed in. This spiral was unfamiliar, not like the episodes of panic that I'd had through my childhood. This was different.

Why can't I breathe?

Braden turned back to the hunt for another lizard, and I closed my eyes, rubbed my hands on my shorts as the July heat just seemed to magnify what was happening inside of me. More weight settled in, and something like terror came with it. My breath drew shorter and shorter, and I tried not to hyperventilate. I opened my eyes, and all I could see were the stars from the lack of oxygen. The sun shone on the surface of the Sacramento River in the distance, and it grew whiter and whiter until it was near-blinding. I closed my eyes again, tried to take another breath but I felt like I lost another inch of my lungs. The invisible fist tightened. The weight on my chest doubled.

This is the anatomy of a crash.

I called Braden, told him we were out of time. I turned and walked to the truck, and he called to me over my shoulder.

"We just got here, Dad," he said. Then he asked, "Five more minutes?"

I didn't respond; instead, I fumbled for the keys in my pocket, then dropped them on the pavement. Bending to pick them up, beads of sweat broke across my forehead and my head swam. I put my hands on my knees, tried to get a grip. It wasn't happening.

Braden caught up to me, talking about the plastic container of lizards and frogs that he had caught. I nodded, said something about the largest lizard, then pushed the button to unlock the truck doors. We climbed in, and while Braden buckled his seatbelt, I reached for my phone and texted Jenn. My thumbs were heavy as I typed.

"Something's wrong with me. We're coming home. Please pray." She texted back and asked what it was, but I didn't respond. I didn't want to acknowledge what I was feeling.

I pulled from the parking lot and wished I were anywhere but here. Braden stared at the lizards in his container, hummed along with the music on the radio. He fidgeted with the lid, cracked it, then closed it, then cracked it again. Every sound amplified, every smell, too.

"Braden, will you stop opening and closing the container, buddy?" I asked.

I sped down 299, putting more distance between us and the river as I ran from something.

Why can't I breathe?

I turned the music off, tried to sing some familiar worship song. I knew the power of worship. I knew how it could bring breakthrough. My earliest memories were marked by this, and in my teenage and early adult years, it had saved my life. When God showed up, nothing was impossible. Demonic attacks, fear, panic—no darkness could stand in His Presence. But even though I knew this truth, even though I'd just finished teaching at our annual summer worship school just two days before, I couldn't seem to get enough breath in my lungs to sing. My chest was on fire.

Am I working myself into a panic? Why?

There was no reason for the panic. By all accounts, things were better than they'd been in years. Jenn, Joel Taylor and I had a dream to create a music label that had a new model that would create excellent worship music and support healthy marriages and families. It didn't even seem possible, yet somehow, it was growing. A handful of our songs had caught fire and were being sung all over the world. Our team was growing, and things were starting to take off. And with the growing success of Bethel Music, more opportunity came. I was co-writing around the clock, working with artists from all over. But with growth and success come complications and challenges. We were creating something new, and it didn't come with a manual. This was new territory for all of us. It was incredible, but it was also intense and challenging. Pioneering something new is exciting, but it can come with misunderstandings. So, even in the midst of all of this blessing, the stress had been growing. It had been simmering just below the surface, and I didn't even realize it was there.

Could I have sensed it if I had stopped long enough to examine the pace of my life? If I had gotten still, would I have realized something was off?

Jenn saw it before I did. She knew I was at the tipping point. She could always see behind my eyes. She saw that I was slammed and disconnected from myself. I was going too fast, moving from one obligation to the next without taking a break. Maybe that's why she suggested I take the afternoon off and take Braden to the river. Maybe she thought I'd find some quiet and catch my breath. It was too little too late, though. It had only been an hour since she'd suggested the trip, and there I was, speeding down the highway, falling apart.

The air in the car seemed thinner. I couldn't stop the thoughts racing through my mind. I wondered whether I'd pass out before I reached the driveway. Braden was oblivious to it all.

Another mile down the highway, and I couldn't shake it. My phone vibrated again and again. I was sure it was Jenn, worried. I gripped the steering wheel but couldn't bring myself to reach for the phone. I was five minutes away from the house.

I just need to get home.

Five minutes seems like an eternity in the middle of a crisis, and as I pulled onto our road, I was fixated on the minute-by-minute changes in my breathing, heart rate, narrowing vision. My mind jumped from one thought to the next. I was only thirty-seven years old. Was I completely losing it?

I threw my truck into park at the end of the driveway and told Braden to go inside and get his mom. "I needed to walk the trails around the house," I told him, and he nodded in agreement. I watched as he ran to the front door, still oblivious to my panic. I opened the truck door without turning off the ignition, and I stepped onto the gravel, legs shaking.

I paced toward the trail, somehow outside of myself, unattached. My head felt like it was floating above me and my hands shook. The weight in the center of my chest was crushing, and I reached for air but couldn't find any. My lungs were frozen. I couldn't push the weight up and off. I tried to slow everything down, tried to take measured breaths, but I couldn't get on top of this torment. There was no air. Staring at the ground, roasting under the afternoon sun, I saw water spots in the dirt. I was crying, my tears falling on the ground, and I couldn't have stopped them if I wanted to. There was no way to control this surge of feelings.

Some kind of similar panic first hit when I was around Braden's age. At only seven, the fear that I might be demonized came on my life; crazy panic and anxiety followed me for almost fifteen years. But I'd beaten that anxiety and panic so many years ago. I'd finally found freedom from that torment. Worship kept everything in balance, kept me sane. But today was different.

The front door slammed, and I looked toward the house. Jenn was running from the porch and down the trail. The air was thinning, and the world began to spin. Still hunched over, I tried to push the anxiety back and stand upright, but I couldn't. Vertigo set in, and I hunched back to my knees. I was afraid to stand up until I felt Jenn's arms wrapped around me. She pulled me up, supported me under the shoulders. She asked whether I was okay, asked what was happening.

"Something is off, physically, mentally. I can't breathe. I can't do it anymore," I said.

"Do what?" she asked, voice trembling. I couldn't find an answer, so I asked her to stay with me, to walk with me. She grabbed my hand, and we started to walk the trail around our property. We didn't go inside. Neither of us wanted our kids to be scared of what was happening.

We walked the trails for what seemed like forever. Jenn sang, and we prayed, but the loop was unrelenting. "Babe, I feel like I'm losing my mind,"

I told her. I was crying uncontrollably and my heart pounded in a runaway rhythm.

"Slow down. Just breathe. It will be okay. You're alright." she said.

I was scaring her, she said. I'm scaring myself, I said. I needed help.

"Maybe you're having a heart attack?" she asked.

My heart was beating so fast I thought it might explode, but I told her I didn't think it was a heart attack. How could I know, though? This was different from anything I'd ever experienced. This was hell.

I didn't answer Jenn's question. Instead, I stared at her, trying to get a full breath.

"Let's go inside and call your parents," she said. We walked toward the house, and she immediately reached for her phone. I could only make out parts of the conversation but realized she was speaking with my dad, telling him what was happening.

"Yeah," she said. "And would you call Kris and Kathy? I'll call Mark."

Jenn hung up the phone, made another call. Then she told me to hold tight. My parents, my friend and trained first-responder, Mark Mack, Kris and Kathy Vallotton, the associate leaders of the church—they were all on the way.

I walked through the front door and into the living room, where worship music was already playing. I turned it up, then knelt down by the speakers and stared out the window. I was desperate for something to take away this nightmare I was stuck in. Jenn stood, phone still to her ear. "Something's really wrong with Brian," she said. "He's crashing. I think maybe it's panic, like when he was younger?"

I remembered the days of my childhood panic and the lessons my dad taught me about breaking these cycles of fear. "When any attack comes," he said, "fight it by saying the name of Jesus, the blood of Jesus, the promises of Scripture and by worshiping God." It was the worship that always worked for me, so I scrolled through my phone and chose a specific playlist, worship songs that I had a history with. I was desperate, and these songs had always helped me find peace in the past. I turned the volume up again, and the music filled the living room.

The music flooded over me, and I concentrated on the truths in the songs. I did everything I knew to do, and still there was no relief. The kids—Haley, Téa, and Braden—watched from the kitchen, eyes wide as Jenn tried to explain to them what was happening to me. They were all so scared but still started praying for me. Haley walked into the living room, put her arms around me and asked if everything was going to be okay. I tried to reassure her, tried to tell her help was coming. She knew I wasn't okay. Haley was cursed with a front-row seat to her dad's meltdown. I was losing it right in front of her eyes.

Song after song, and still nothing changed. Jenn walked in from the kitchen, tried to hug me again, but my senses were overloading. Through tears, I told her I couldn't handle this kind of torment much longer.

Trapped in the overwhelming panic, I wasn't able to connect to anything or anyone. I felt completely alone and hopeless. Behind my eyes, I sensed the void. It was terrifying. There was only darkness, and I was falling too far, too fast. My shirt was soaked through, and my thoughts were scattered. My heart was beating in triple time.

I felt like I was sliding into insanity.

TWO

AWAKENINGS

* * *

In the 1970s my dad had worked under my grandpa at Bethel Church in Redding, California. He'd started the Salt House, a ministry outreach to the hippies living in Redding during the Jesus Movement. He had a heart for the people who didn't fit into traditional church environments, and as he poured into them, he saw God begin to move. There was an anointing on his life that was evident.

My dad loved working with my grandpa, but in 1978 he was invited to pastor a little church in the mountains an hour west of Redding. Both my grandpa and my dad felt like it was an open door from God. So when I was only six months old, my parents left Redding and were sent to Mountain Chapel in Weaverville, California.

My brother Eric, sister Leah and I made our earliest memories in that tiny town. The great outdoors were just beyond our backyard, and Eric and I spent most of our time there, exploring the woods, catching lizards, building forts and searching for our next adventure. In our front yard we played baseball, football and just about every other sport with the neighborhood kids. Whether I was with family, friends or by myself, you could always find me where I felt the most alive—outside.

My childhood was filled with memories of my family. I couldn't imagine better parents, and I told my parents just about everything. Growing up in the house of a pastor, I guess it should come as no surprise that I cannot remember a time when I didn't know about God. My mom and dad taught us the stories of the Bible and showed us how to pray. It was never a big production; it was just a part of our everyday life. And before he was a pastor, my dad was a worship leader, so he taught us the importance of worship both at church and in our home. "Worship was the main event," he said, "because worship connects us to God in a way nothing else can." He told us that we were never too young to connect with God because there is no junior Holy Spirit.

Even in my earliest memories, I knew I could have my own relationship with God. God's Presence could show up anywhere, and we were raised to recognize Him. My mom was an early riser, and she'd wake up before all of us so she could have her morning devotions. As a mom of three kids, it was the only time of day that she had alone. But she wasn't the only early riser, and I always seemed to know when she was up. Even at the age of three, there were so many mornings I'd see the light coming from the living room, and I'd crawl from my bed and walk down the carpeted hall to the living room. I'd find her there, sitting on the couch with her Bible, praying and spending time with God.

While those times were her only time alone all day, she'd still pull me up and let me sit with her. I wasn't the most affectionate kid, but my mom always managed to break through. She'd kiss me on the forehead and pull me closer. I'd lean in, pull my yellow and white checkered Winnie-the-Pooh blanket to my chest and stick my thumb in my mouth while she continued her devotions.

It never occurred to me until I had kids of my own, but I was interrupting my mom's time with God. She could have seen me as an intrusion, but instead she invited me into those moments, where she showed me the power of simple devotion by living it out. I was daily shown something rather than having her explain what was happening, but even at that young age, I knew that it was special. Those moments birthed something inside of me.

Weaverville is a very small town of just a few thousand, the kind where everyone knew everyone. My parents weren't just pastors at the church; they were involved in our community, and though they set boundaries to protect family time, our doors were often open. We often had families from the church and community coming over to our house, and when they did, our parents would have us to go outside and play so that they could talk. But when the weather didn't cooperate, we'd end up playing indoors.

I couldn't have been more than four, and we were playing hide-and-seek inside. I was hiding in a bedroom closet when I was found. I ran through the kitchen as my brother chased me. In the hall, I could hear his footsteps were right behind me. Eric was gaining, about to catch me, when a door flew open and smacked me on the forehead. It knocked me right off my feet, and the back of my head hit the floor as stars flashed in my eyes. Seconds passed, and eventually the ceiling came back into focus. Everything hurt, and I looked up to find our family friend, Kathy Vallotton, standing over me. She asked if I was okay, but I didn't answer. I simply stood up, pushed back any thought of pain, and gritted my teeth so I wouldn't cry. I didn't let anyone know that I was hurt. I was tough.

Years later, Kathy would tell me that I never cried, not even when I was hurt. I might have had a high pain tolerance, but in the coming years I'd come to know a new type of pain that I couldn't imagine.

———————————————————

Not long after the hide-and-seek incident, I was sitting in the back of our blue Toyota hatchback. We were headed down the mountain to Redding to see my grandparents, and my parents were in the front of the car, singing worship songs. Dropping out of the mountains and into a pass, we hit a straight stretch of road, and that's when it happened. There was an intensity in the car, something I'd never experienced. It was a holy moment, a moment where heaven seemed to come close, and I'd never felt anything like it. It was the Presence of God—I knew it, even at four years old—but this time, I was experiencing it firsthand, and it had come out of nowhere. I could sense something stirring inside of me, and it was holy. The air in the car was thick, and I felt something inside of me change. A feeling came over me, a feeling I'd never experienced, and I couldn't help but respond. I started speaking in another language, a language I couldn't understand but also couldn't hold in. It was the first time I spoke in tongues.

In that mountain pass, God became real to me in a whole new way. I hadn't done anything to make this happen, hadn't tried to force it, and there'd been no fear, only peace and joy. It was the purest, most undeniable experience of God. Heaven came down into that car, and it was impossible to deny. I had an experience with God that couldn't be contrived. We kept on driving, and eventually the moment passed. I was marked that day, and it's still a part of me.

———————————————————

I'd been awakened by this encounter with God, but as I got older there were other awakenings. When I was seven, a neighborhood girl my age would come over, and we'd play a lot in the backyard. We were close friends and often explored the woods together.

One summer day, we were playing out of the eyesight of my parents. We ran toward a pile of rocks in our backyard and that's when our curiosity got the best of us. I wondered about the differences between boys and girls, and she was every bit as curious as I was. We knew it was wrong, but we decided to do it anyway. I moved in to kiss her, and she kissed me back. It felt good, and so we took the next step and showed each other what made us different. In that moment, my stomach turned, and something awoke.

I knew it was wrong. Something told me not to do it, but I ignored that small voice and pushed it down. But there, as the reality of our decision sunk in, guilt and shame filled me.

I sprinted through the back door of my house, knowing I'd done something wrong. And though I'd broken the rules before, somehow this was different. It was the first time I felt the weight and intensity of real guilt. I had to tell my mom; I couldn't wait.

I found her napping on the couch, but I couldn't let her sleep. I shook her awake, told her everything just as it had happened. She didn't offer much of a response, just nodded and told me to go play, and I wondered if she had heard me. Shouldn't she have been angry or upset? Shouldn't her response have matched the guilt I was feeling?

Later that evening, I told her again, just to make sure she understood how sorry I was. She still didn't blow up or freak out. I was going to be okay, she said. She saw that I was sorry for what I had done, and she said if I still felt the weight of guilt, I should go straight to God and let Him know how sorry I was for what I had done. He would forgive me.

I went to my room, still feeling the weight from what I had done that afternoon. But I took my mom's advice and turned to God, telling Him how sorry I was. As soon as I prayed, as soon as I repented, the guilt fell away. And that's when I realized that I was accountable to both my parents and God for my actions. I also realized I had a choice as to how I'd live my life. I could choose right or wrong, but if I chose to do what I knew was wrong, I'd suffer the consequences of guilt and shame. It was repenting that brought the freedom from guilt.

I'd experienced freedom in that moment, so I made a habit of sharing the harder things with my mom over the years. After school, we'd all sit in the kitchen and talk about our days. I'd tell her everything, the highs and lows, even when I'd broken the rules. She was quick with encouragement and forgiveness but never lowered the standard. She smiled a lot and laughed a lot too. When I needed it, she'd call me out on bad decisions, but she would always follow it with an understanding word, and though I didn't always welcome it, she was quick with a hug, too.

My dad was just as affectionate as my mom. Every night he came into our rooms and prayed over each of us. He never missed a night, even though there were some nights he'd come in really late, thinking we were asleep. On those nights, I'd pretend to be out cold, and I'd listen as he prayed over me. He'd pray protection over me and that I would always have a heart for the Lord. He prayed for my future, for my wife and for the man I would become someday. These weren't quick prayers. He took his time night after night as he prayed for us, and as I'd listen, his words would lull me to sleep.

My parents raised us right. They raised us to love God and people, to have fun and to do our best. And though a lot of pastors' kids were expected to act, dress or perform a certain way, my mom and dad never put that kind of pressure on any of us. They never pressured us in school, either. When we brought our report cards home, they'd look first at our conduct and then at our Bible grades. If those were good, they didn't worry much about the other grades as long as we promised we'd done our best. They always said that if our conduct and Bible grades were good, the rest would usually follow.

My parents felt it was important to let us be kids, but they helped us understand the important things in life. We were only disciplined for having a bad attitude or poor behavior. My dad made sure we understood we were responsible for our actions, and if we made a mess or hurt someone, it was our job to make it right. They raised us to understand the impact of right and wrong choices in life. And though my parents were quick to assure me of God's love and forgiveness when I chose to do wrong, they didn't pretend like there weren't very real consequences when I chose to do wrong. There was discipline when we deserved it and grace when we repented and cleaned up the messes we made.

These were lessons I'd lean into as I grew older, and I'd need to learn and relearn. I didn't know I'd have to learn these lessons in a much deeper way in my mid-thirties. I'd have to trace a line back through my history and go back to some of those fundamental truths and clean up some of messes I made.

THREE

THE FOUR WEAPONS

* * *

The terror started when I was just seven years old. It came fast, unexpected, and out of nowhere. It was like nothing I'd ever seen or experienced, and at first, I didn't notice any specific trigger. It was just terrifying.

As pastor's kids, Eric, Leah and I were in church whenever the doors were open. "We don't *have* to go to church," my dad said. "We *get* to go." And the truth is, we actually enjoyed it. I went to most of the kids' events, and it was at one of those gatherings—a children's small group meeting—when it first started. It was the moment everything changed, and my eyes were opened to an invisible world.

In a room full of energetic first-graders, I was sitting with my friends and we were singing a song. The kids' worship pastor was sitting in a chair across from me, singing songs and asking us to clap along. Even as a kid, I knew the songs I liked and the songs I didn't, and this one fell into the *didn't-like* category. I thought it was dumb, and I was embarrassed to sing along.

He started another verse, and that's when the air around me changed. It was as if someone opened a door, letting in a cold draft. A presence filled the room, but this presence wasn't holy, and it certainly wasn't the Presence

I'd experienced in the car or at my mom's side in those early mornings. There was no joy, and there was no peace in it either. This presence was different. It was dark, and I knew immediately it was evil.

The hair on the back of my neck stood up, and goosebumps started to break out down my arms as a cold sweat broke out across my forehead. I was immediately filled with terror. I had seen people manifest demons while being prayed over at church, but the truth is, I never really thought much about it. It was something that happened from time to time during an altar call when people came forward to receive prayer, but in that moment the thought that I could be possessed by a demon became a real fear for the first time.

I thought about those people who manifested at church, how they jerked and shook, and though I wasn't doing any of those things, I worried that I might at any moment. On the inside, I felt the way those who manifested looked on the outside—out of control, overwhelmed, terrified. The terror was building, and that's when the question set in.

Could a demon manifest in me?

I couldn't seem to push away the fear that an evil spirit might take over my body. It was such a scary thought, and it played over and over in my head. I was losing my grip and sinking under waves of fear.

I thought I should pray but didn't know what to say. What if the fear overwhelmed me? What if I lost control in front of everyone? My friends kept on singing, clapping on rhythm and laughing. They weren't experiencing the terror that was growing heavier by the minute. Why was I? How could I make it stop?

The darkness was all around me, and I wanted to hide. There was only one problem: there was nowhere to hide. My heart kept pounding, and I knew that I was too little to fight this alone. I felt trapped, like I couldn't escape, but I looked over my shoulder and saw a clear path to the door, so I did the only thing I could think to do. I ran from the fear, straight into the bathroom.

I locked the door, bent over the sink and took one deep breath, then another. This was something beyond me, and I was confused and scared, overwhelmed by all the feelings inside of me. I turned to the mirror and stared into my eyes, searching for something out of the ordinary, something that might explain what was going on. I'd heard that if a demon possessed someone, you could tell by looking in their eyes. I looked and looked, but I didn't see anything. My eyes weren't bloodshot, and there was no evil face looking back at me. But if I wasn't demonized, why was I so afraid? Where had all that fear come from? Nothing had happened to cause this sudden terror, but it was unshakable.

Nothing made sense, and I didn't feel safe. I couldn't shake the fear though that I had a demon; and if I stayed in that house, if I didn't leave that bathroom, I might lose it altogether. I needed my mom and dad, so without a second thought I bolted from the house.

I ran as fast as I could, and as I sprinted through the streets of Weaverville, my world began closing in and collapsing on me. The sky pressed down on my heart, which had been racing even before I started running, and it felt as if it might explode. The terror was just behind me, chasing me down the street. I knew it.

I ran through the door of my house, crossed into the living room, and doubled over, gasping for air. My dad was there, and he stood from the couch and asked what was wrong. I sobbed and stammered, tried to tell him something was happening, but I couldn't get the words out. He didn't need any words, though, because the panic in my eyes told the story. He knew this wasn't normal kid stuff. Something was desperately wrong, and I needed his help.

My dad didn't waste any time, and he started to fight for me. It was an all-out war, and his generally quiet demeanor gave way to something more fierce, something more militant. He took authority over the evil presence and commanded it to stop tormenting me with bold and aggressive prayers, but even as he prayed, the fear wouldn't let go. It held onto me.

That's when he started to worship. He sang the songs I knew by heart, songs we sang at church almost every Sunday. But the way he sang those songs wasn't soft and gentle. He sang them with the same boldness of his prayers, directly to the heart of God.

Nothing seemed to change, not at first. Even though I knew my dad was with me, the fear was unrelenting. As the minutes passed, I began to think it might never end, but my dad kept singing and didn't let up. Ten minutes passed, then twenty. Finally, thirty minutes in, the overwhelming terror broke. I'd been trapped inside a hell I didn't create, and thirty minutes after my dad starting singing and praying for me, that hellish feeling left my body. I knew the peace that passes all understanding, and I was filled with gratitude. It was as if heaven came down and took over, just like it had in the car when I was four.

The torment was gone. What I thought might lead to death hadn't, and I was finally safe again with my parents. I wasn't consumed by the terror anymore, and my heartbeat regulated. I could breathe. I was alive.

———————————————

The night at children's small group was one I would never forget, and after it, everything was different. I grew more sensitive to the spiritual world, and I could sense the Presence of God and the presence of evil.

The church was experiencing a move of God in those days, and more and more people were coming to experience Him in a very real way. They were finding salvation, healing and deliverance. They were actually finding freedom. But after my first experience with the demonic, a church event became a potential place for my terror to happen.

There were some Sundays full of spiritual warfare in my childhood, but there's one Sunday I'll never forget. My dad was preaching, and when he finished, he invited people to respond, to come forward if they needed prayer. The response to the invitation was overwhelming, just like it had been on so many Sundays before. People poured out of their seats and made their way forward. I stood by my mom, and her eyes were closed as she prayed for the people coming to the front.

My dad stood with the rest of the prayer team as people lined up for prayer. The worship team started to play, and I could feel something change in the room. It was powerful, and even at that age, I knew God was doing something special.

Out of nowhere, a woman screamed as if she was being attacked by some invisible force. She fell to the ground and started shaking. Her arms stiffened, then her legs. Was she in pain? Her eyes widened, and she looked like she was trapped inside of a waking nightmare. I was close enough to touch her, but I didn't dare. Something dark surrounded her, and I didn't want it to attack me. I could feel the fear starting to build in my stomach.

My dad and a couple of people from the prayer team knelt next to the woman, and they spoke the name of Jesus over her before starting to pray quietly. It took just a few minutes before her face completely changed, and she stopped crying. I watched as peace seemed to come over her, and she closed her eyes and smiled. Her torment was over. Peace had come. But even though this woman had been delivered, all I felt was fear.

As we pulled out of the parking lot after the service, I was relieved the experience was over. I'd gotten out of the church building without being sucked into my own nightmare of fear. I'd avoided another episode of panic, and it felt like nothing short of a miracle.

That evening, I asked my dad how a person becomes possessed. He tried to explain in words that a seven-year-old would understand. He explained that sometimes there's a voice, a dark influence in a person's life that encourages them to do wrong, and over time, that voice leads them down a path further and further away from God.

"But a demonic influence can't stay in your life if you don't want it to," he said.

I'd received Jesus into my heart and been filled with the Holy Spirit. I had parents who were praying over me. Still, I wondered whether a demon could take control of me, and my dad must have known what I was thinking because he told me not to worry. While I might be tormented, I wasn't possessed. God had given me the tools to stay connected to Him and to fight against those dark forces. God would protect me.

My dad gave me assurances I could understand at that age. He'd spoken words that helped me overcome the irrational fears that had come over me. I'd hold onto those words for years to come.

———————————————————

Weeks passed, and I joined my dad for the regular Friday night prayer meeting. It started with worship, just like any other prayer meeting. There was no agenda other than to worship, and in that atmosphere we searched for God's heart, asked Him where He wanted to take us that night. As the music played, some of the people in the service stood. Some sat. Some were face down on the floor in worship. Within minutes, we could feel His Presence with us.

It was an unusual night, one of those times when the Presence of God was strong, and as we sang, a woman whom we'd never seen walked into the room, and she was loud and disruptive. She was rambling and abrasive, and she brought something dark with her. And though the room was unified in praise and worship before she came in, she was causing a disruption.

Within minutes she went from being mildly disruptive to completely flipping out. There was no doubt about it—she was demonized—and a couple of people came around her. They tried to calm her down, and as they did, I felt that familiar fear start to rise up in my stomach. There was a battle in the spirit realm, and even though I was only seven, I could sense it. I knew the enemy was trying to disrupt a holy moment.

I wasn't the only one who sensed it, though. The devil had overplayed his hand and had taken it too far with this woman. It was evident to all of us. But what was meant to be a distraction actually took us deeper into God. The room moved as one, and our worship and prayer became even more intense and focused. Our praise went higher and wider and deeper. And though the panic was crouching close by, though it was just outside me, it wasn't attacking me. Somehow, I knew God was protecting me.

I joined in the worship, and even though I could feel the chaos around me, it never overtook me. The Presence of God was so powerful and present during that meeting. I knew God would protect me. I'd never been more certain of anything.

In that atmosphere of focused worship, that darkness never stood a chance. After a few songs, the woman was delivered from her torment. She stopped screaming and crying, and her body relaxed as she fell into a deep rest. I could feel peace enter the room, and I came to understand that in an atmosphere of worship, in a place where God is present, the enemy has no power.

The attacks of terror and fear weren't uncommon in those days. They had this ability to grip me at any moment. Sometimes I'd win those battles, but other times, the fear got the best of me.

So often, the fear came at night. I'd stare at the black ceiling and wonder whether I might see a demon, or maybe even the devil himself, and my thoughts would spin out of control. Some nights, I couldn't seem to pull it together. The fear escalated and turned to terror. Terror was too big a weight, and it settled on my chest, threatening to crush me and pull me down.

There were times the terror became so thick that I lost control. I'd pull myself from my bed and run down the hallway, hoping some demon wouldn't open the closet door and knock me off my feet. In those moments the hallway was never-ending, but when I finally reached the end of it, I'd turn to the staircase, run up, and turn down another pitch-black hallway that led to my parents' bedroom. Fear chased me the whole way, and when I finally reached their door, I'd scream out, "It's happening again!"

I'd run to their bed and jump right in between them, crouching down on my knees. My dad would sit up, grab my shoulders, pull me up, and look into my eyes. His eyes were kind but intense, and he would tell me I was going to be okay. But as true as those words were, they didn't feel true in that moment. The terror that stalked me in the middle of the night was too much, and it threatened to consume me.

Being so young, I didn't understand how to battle this fear when it descended. It wasn't some bad dream my dad could wake me from or some overreaction he could talk me through. This was a real thing—a demonic attack that had to be fought. He started by saying the name of Jesus. He didn't just chant it over me, though. He declared the name. He knew that Jesus' name spoken in faith had power. If the fear didn't break, he'd plead the blood of Jesus over me. He'd claim that no demonic force could withstand His blood. He'd declare the blood over and over, and odd as this should have sounded in my childhood, maybe even scary, it wasn't. It gave me some small measure of comfort.

When the attacks persisted, and I sank deeper into my own fear, my dad reached for verses that he had memorized. He'd declare them over me as promises that were mine, but if that didn't work to bring me freedom, he'd start to worship, and usually that is when everything would start to change. Most nights, it was worship that would start to bring relief. The overwhelming heaviness would lift, and heaven would come. And once the intensity started to lift, he'd have me sing with him. He understood the importance of these moments. He couldn't be the only one fighting; I needed to learn that I had a role to play too.

Those nights replayed again and again. On some occasions, the terror passed quickly, but on other nights, it lasted so long my mom would take her pillow and go to the couch while my dad kept fighting. He'd fight until the panic broke, and for as long as I could remember he used the same four weapons—worship, the blood of Jesus, the name of Jesus, and the Word of God.

In the early days, my dad didn't teach me the theological principles of fighting back the spiritual attacks. Instead, he simply did the work to fight for my freedom when I was caught in those moments of chaos.

When I wasn't lost in the panic, my parents taught me each of those core principles so I might come to understand the power each had in my life. They taught me that when you're fighting an ongoing spiritual attack, God is using those moments to train you for war, to learn how to gain authority in that area of life that's under attack.

———————————————————————

Four years passed and though I had intense moments of fear, my childhood was mostly normal. I played outside and explored the woods. I played baseball, basketball and football. I ran around with friends. I did the things normal kids do. Even though there were seasons when the fear set in nightly, there were times when I might go weeks without an episode. But as these attacks came and went, I started noticing the key to my relief: worship. It was the thing that broke the torment and brought me peace.

My dad taught me about the power of worship in those early years, and he did it by fighting for me. But I often wondered what would happen if the panic fell when my dad wasn't around. Would I know what to do?

I made the annual trip to Mount Lassen camp with the children's group from our church. I loved going to camp as a kid. There was a creek that we would go swimming and fishing in. There were baseball fields and cabins and a wood-sided barn for our meetings. Still, I carried fear with me to camp, because if I had an episode, my parents wouldn't be there to help me through it.

We gathered in the barn for an evening session, and we sang all the songs I loved. When the worship time was over, the visiting preacher spoke—about what, I can't remember—and when he was finished, he invited anyone to come forward who wanted more of God. It was an invitation he'd extended every night, but I hadn't responded. That night, though, I felt the pull, and so I walked to the front, my friends following behind me. One of the adults came to me, put his hands on my shoulders, and prayed. I closed my eyes, and listened to his prayer. Around us, others were laughing and crying, and as he kept praying, an unexplainable joy came over me. It filled my body, and I knew I needed to lie down on the sawdust floor. As I did, I sensed God all around me, filling the space, filling me.

As it turned out, I wasn't the only one who sensed God's Presence. Around the room, kids were being touched by God. They were falling out in His Presence and speaking in tongues. A girl to my left was lying on the floor crying, and as she kept crying, I could feel a deep sadness on her. Her tears turned into sobs, and I knew she must be dealing with something heavy.

Some adults surrounded her and started to pray, but she only cried harder as more pain seemed to fill her. This sort of thing would normally spiral me into fear, but something was different. I sensed I'd be safe if I stayed right where I was, on my back, remaining completely vulnerable. I knew I didn't have to put up any guards to try to protect myself. I only needed to stay in that moment with God, to worship Him and trust that He would keep the fear and panic away. And as I surrendered to that truth, God was faithful. The terror never touched me.

It was a powerful moment, and it became a major moment of hope. God had shown me I could fight the panic and terror even when there wasn't someone around to help me. It was an anchor I would need in the days to come.

———

Over the years, through my dad's teaching, I've come to understand the four weapons he used to fight the attacks of the enemy—the name of Jesus, the blood of Jesus, the Word of God, and worship. He never used those weapons randomly. Instead, he discerned what was needed in the moment, and he used that tool.

In time, I came to understand exactly why my dad used those tools. I heard him preach about the blood of Jesus, how it carries authority and weight and how we have been given authority through His name to come against any attack. I began to understand how Jesus' name brings freedom. I watched as my dad prayed for people and healing came in the name of Jesus, just like Peter did in the book of Acts.

> Then Peter said, "Silver or gold I do not have, but what I do
> have I give you. In the name of Jesus Christ of Nazareth,
> walk." (Acts 3:6)

And in my own life, I experienced the power of the statement in the book of Luke:

> "Lord, even the demons submit to us in your name."
> (Luke 10:17)

I came to know the power of Jesus' blood, too. I learned the truth of Isaiah 53:5:

> But He was wounded for our transgressions,
> He was bruised for our iniquities;
> The chastisement for our peace was upon Him,
> And by His stripes we are healed.

Peter used this same truth in the New Testament, writing, "Our instant healing flowed from his wounding" (1 Peter 2:24), and I learned that the word "healing" there—*sozo*—doesn't just mean physical healing. It means salvation, healing, and deliverance. So, all those years ago my dad was praying for complete healing of my spirit, soul, and body.

The power of the Word of God is undeniable. It's not just words on a page. It is alive and active, speaking to me about any situation that I'm going through. Scripture is the very word of God and has the power through

His Spirit to turn any situation around. As Brian Simmons once said, "Only those who touch the Scriptures in faith receive its promises." As I grew in the understanding of my faith, I experienced that truth. I learned that "Not one promise from God is empty of power, for with God there is no such thing as impossibility" (Luke 1:37) and that "All Scripture is God-breathed..." (2 Timothy 3:16). There are anchors in the Bible, and in different seasons, different scriptures came to life for me. They steadied me and gave me the courage to walk through difficult and sometimes painful times.

As powerful as these tools were—the name of Jesus, the blood of Jesus and the Word of God—worship was the tool I used the most. So often, it brought complete relief, and over time, I realized the truth Morris Smith once preached: "Real worship defies definition, it can only be experienced. Worship was never intended by God to be the discussion of textbooks but rather the communion with God experienced by His loved ones."

I leaned into this truth: worship is more than singing songs to God; it's investing in our relationship with Him, even when we don't feel like it or when circumstances are difficult. Worship acknowledges those difficulties and turns to God regardless. When we worship, we declare who God is and who we are through Him.

I'd built my life around worship and had experienced the power of God. But in the hours after I'd returned from the river with Braden, worship didn't seem to bring the breakthrough. Maybe it was because this episode was different from the panic of my childhood. Sure, there were some similarities: the panic came out of nowhere; it snuck up on me; it was unrelenting. But for all the similarities, it also felt so different. My childhood panic seemed connected to some larger spiritual reality. The attack that had started at the river wasn't connected to anything spiritual, at least not as far as I could tell. Maybe that's why those familiar tools didn't seem to be working.

In the house, I struggled to get a breath and wondered what was happening. I desperately needed some kind of relief, but it wasn't coming. And if I'd have known that freedom wouldn't come for another six months, I'm not sure I would have made it.

FOUR

THE SPIRAL

* * *

I paced the living room floor, and my breathing grew even shallower. Jenn asked if it felt like one of the attacks of my childhood. "It was different," I told her. She asked how, but I couldn't say. I told her I couldn't get on top of the panic, couldn't seem to catch my breath.

"Try to slow down," she said.

My thoughts were cloudy, and I couldn't seem to put a rational thought together. Was I losing my mind? I needed God to deliver me from whatever this was. I needed to believe peace could spring up just as quickly as the panic had set in by the river.

Spiraling as I was, breathless as I was, I did my best to sing along with the worship music playing over the house speakers. I'd experienced the power of worship so many times in my life and experienced firsthand the freedom it brought. But in this moment of new need, nothing seemed to be working.

This has to stop. I can't breathe. I'm suffocating.

I was kneeling on the floor by the window, face to the ground, when I heard my dad's voice. I looked up, saw them all there in the kitchen. I don't remember them walking in, but they were standing with Kris and Kathy, surrounding Jenn, asking her questions. They turned and walked into the living room.

It might have been an hour since I'd come home, or it could have been an eternity. I had no idea. I was disconnected from time. I asked my parents how long they'd been at the house, and my mom said it'd been fifteen minutes. How had I not seen them for fifteen minutes? *Everything is slipping*, I thought.

My mom repeated Jenn's question and asked if this was like what I experienced as a child. I told her it was different. I hadn't been afraid of spiritual attacks for over fifteen years, and this wasn't the same. This was something else, something like my world crashing in on itself. Everything was collapsing, and though there might have been some spiritual component—isn't there always?—this was something more physical. Something was off in my body.

Another rush came, another surge of something that felt like adrenaline. It rushed over me without warning, and I was pulled deeper into a growing pit. The air in the living room felt charged with electricity, and I clenched my fists and gritted my teeth, hoping I could stop it through sheer will.

Nothing changed.

Kris came to me and told me that I'd be okay. He'd been through his own torment, a nervous breakdown where he had eventually found freedom, and his words gave me some small bit of comfort. Still pacing, still searching for balance, I turned to the window. How many hours had passed by?

My heart pounded against my chest in rhythm like it might rupture. I turned back from the window and noticed Mark, a retired fire captain and family friend. I had no idea how long he had been there. He was talking to Jenn in the kitchen, and for the first time, I noticed how her eyes were red and heavy. Her shoulders were drooping. She was carrying this weight with me. She listened to Mark and nodded along. Mark reached for his phone and headed outside.

Jenn came into the room and took my hand. She told me the ambulance was on its way. "Everything is going to be okay," she said. I knew this was the kind of thing people say when they're trying to convince themselves. She was trying to convince both of us.

The EMT materialized just like everyone else had in the past few hours. This was really happening. I turned to Jenn, looked into her eyes and asked her to pray. Over her shoulder, I saw my kids, huddled up, crying, scared. There was an electric intensity in the air, and it buzzed through us all.

But then a divine moment of clarity cut through and caught me off guard. For the past couple of hours, I'd been in survival mode while everyone moved around me and tried to take care of me. For the first time since this started at the river, I saw the smallest light of hope at the end of a very dark tunnel. That hint of light didn't grow, but it was enough, and in that moment, I felt like I had to make a declaration of faith over myself and my family. The pressure settled heavier on my chest, but I walked to my kids, pulled them close, and said, "This is when God becomes real."

It was the truest thing to say in the moment. I knew I had to draw a line in the sand and then step over it. I tried to remind myself of my own history and remember how God had always met me in my most desperate moments, how He'd always been faithful to me. And even though this moment felt hopeless, even though I didn't know when or how it'd resolve, this step of faith sent a message to my kids. I couldn't shield them from the reality of my breaking. I didn't even want to. I wanted them to see my breaking so they could see me choose to believe God. They needed to experience what only God can do. God becomes real in a whole new way when He becomes your only option, and they would need this moment to realize that truth. It would become an anchor for their own faith.

It was one of the biggest moments of trust that I have ever chosen. Even today, trying to put words to it is difficult because words don't do justice to the significance and power of it.

The EMT led me to the kitchen table and asked me to sit. He took my pulse and held a stethoscope to my chest and listened to my breathing. He called out my vitals. I didn't know what the different numbers meant, but my heart was racing, and the EMTs seemed nervous as they worked fast.

He turned to his partner and asked for something, and the second EMT left the room. Moments later, he came back into the kitchen wheeling an oxygen tank. He handed me a clear plastic mask, and I held it over my nose and mouth as they turned the knob. The oxygen flowed, and I took the deepest breath I could. Finally I felt air filling my lungs for the first time in hours. There was a small glimmer of hope.

There was a prick in my forearm as they put in an IV. The EMT pumped something through that IV, and whatever it was, it was a miracle. For the first time in hours, everything slowed down. My body was warming, and my heart wasn't pounding quite so hard. It was a chemical peace, sure, but in that moment I'd take any type of peace I could get.

My heart was still beating too hard and fast, but there was good news. The EMTs didn't think I was having a heart attack. But they still wanted to take me to the hospital for observation. I nodded, stood, and followed them out of the kitchen and through the front door. As they loaded me into the ambulance, I remembered what I'd said to my kids.

This is when God becomes real.

FIVE

MY OWN WEAPON

* * *

The terror came and went all the way into my preteen years, and there was no rhyme or reason to its coming or going. I never knew when it might show up, when it might crash over me. But understanding why the panic came was less important to me than knowing what to do when it did, and with my parents' help I was learning how to handle it.

My parents led by example during those times. They stepped in and took authority over the panic, and they cultivated an atmosphere of worship that drove the terror away. As I grew older, though, my parents started teaching me how to fight for myself. I needed to take personal responsibility for what was happening in my life. I needed to learn the power and authority I carried.

I felt anything but authoritative. I was in junior high, and the fear was spreading into my everyday life. I'd start to panic and feel claustrophobic in cars and elevators. The night brought fear, too, which increased the chances of having an episode at night. In moments of clarity, I knew these fears were irrational, but when the terror came, rational thinking didn't matter. There was no explaining away the fear.

My mom and dad didn't let the fear consume our family. If the panic came during the early evening, my dad would take me to another room to help me through it. Before my mom would join us, she would explain everything to Eric and Leah, tell them I'd be okay and they didn't need to worry. When it was over, they'd reassure us all. "This won't last forever," they'd say. "Eventually you'll win, and the panic will stop."

It was a night like any other, and I sat in the living room with my family in front of the television. I can't remember what we were watching or any of the other small details from that night. What I can tell you is there was no reason it should have happened, nothing that should have brought the fear, but there it was. It broke out across the back of my neck, and the hairs on my arm stood up. Before I could push it back, the memories of when the fear started came flooding in, how the atmosphere changed without warning, and there, surrounded by my family in our well-lit and comfortable living room, that same feeling pressed down on me.

My dad must have seen it, but he didn't make a production of it, and he didn't draw attention to me. Instead, in the most even tone, he asked my mom to start putting Eric and Leah to bed, and he sat on the couch next to me as I tried to keep from falling apart. I couldn't stop the spiral, though. I didn't want to be afraid anymore, but I felt completely helpless. He turned straight to prayer and worship.

Minutes passed, and I felt the grip of fear loosen a little bit. It wasn't much, but it was enough. That's when he turned to me.

"Fight with me," he said. "Let's beat this together."

He knew it was important for me to get my own personal victories, and so he was inviting me to fight my fear with him.

We began singing the simple songs of worship, and even through my tears and shortness of breath, I did my best to sing along. But peace didn't come, so my dad opened his Bible. He asked me to read these verses out loud, declaring these promises over myself:

With God, nothing is impossible. (Luke 1:37)

God has not given you a spirit of fear, but of power, love,
and a sound mind. (2 Timothy 1:7)

The fear still didn't loosen its grip on me, though. In fact, it only seemed to intensify. We turned to worship, and hours passed. I sang as if it might be the last time I'd ever sing to God. I let loose, raised my voice with complete passion and desperation, but I wasn't singing and praying for God to come and rescue me. In that moment of desperation, I was worshiping and thanking God for what I knew He was going to do. I was partnering with God for my breakthrough.

We sang through the night and into the early morning, and God showed His faithfulness. As the early morning light began to come through the window, the air changed in a moment. The blanket of fear was replaced by the peace of the Presence of God. I closed my eyes, and there it was again, that feeling of deep gratitude I'd grown accustomed to after the fear broke. It felt like I'd been pulled straight up from hell. But this time, the breakthrough was richer and fuller.

My dad felt the shift, too, and he turned to me, smiling. "You did it," he said. "You beat this." I'd had his help, but I'd won. It was a night that marked me. Praise had the power to break this unpredictable terror. I knew I could go on the offensive now.

My dad made sure I didn't forget that moment. In the following days, he reminded me how praise and worship had been the key. And this wasn't coincidental; it was biblical. In fact, it was just like the story of King Jehoshaphat.

King Jehoshaphat was the ruler of Judah and Jerusalem, and he had received word from the prophets. The enemy armies of three different people groups—the Ammonites, Moabites, and the people of Mount Seir—were coming to war against him and his people. The enemy armies were bigger, stronger, and larger than the armies of God's people, and they had one goal in mind—total annihilation.

It was a time of terror, of great fear and panic, and the people were desperate for deliverance. Jehoshaphat was afraid, too, and so he called the people to an assembly. On his face, he sought the Lord, declared the power of God, and called upon His name. God alone could rescue them, he said, and that's when he turned to bold prayer, reminding God of the promises He'd made to His people. While he prayed, the spirit of God fell on one of the prophets, and that prophet came forward and delivered the word of God. He told the people not to fear, that the battle was not theirs but God's. The Lord would fight for them. "Go to the battlefield," the prophet said, "and see what God will do."

The next day came, and it was a classic biblical battle scene. True to the word of God delivered by the prophet, Jehoshaphat and the people of Judah and Jerusalem marched toward the enemy armies waiting in the valley. As they moved toward certain war, Jehoshaphat appointed worshipers to go before the army of God, and those worshipers lifted songs, praising Him in advance for the victory He'd promised the day before. When the enemy armies heard the praises of God, a curious thing happened. They descended into chaos, turned on one another, and slaughtered each other. Just like that, the battle was over. The people of God had been rescued without raising a sword. Their deliverance had come by a simple act of thankful praise, an act of faith before it had even happened.

"This is the point of the story," my dad said. "We can fight our darkest fears with nothing more than praise and worship. As God is glorified, atmospheres are shifted when He comes. He eradicates our enemies and drives out our fear. Praise and worship were the things that ushered in the Presence of God and brought freedom." His Presence comes when faith-filled worship is offered to Him. God can't resist that kind of praise.

It was just a couple of weeks before my thirteenth birthday and just a week after that early morning victory. I sat in the living room by my dad, and it was time for bed.

"If anything happens tonight," he said, "try to worship on your own first. But if you feel like you can't handle it, come and get me. I don't want you to feel alone or like you have to handle it by yourself."

I told him I'd come get him if I needed him. He left the living room and made his way up the stairs to his bedroom. I stayed behind, deciding I'd sleep on the living room floor beside the coffee table.

I fell asleep quickly, but hours later, I woke up suddenly. I sat straight up on the floor. The digital clock on the far side of the room told me it was three o'clock in the morning, and there, in those early hours, a chill washed over me. There was a dark presence in the room, and it was sitting right next to me.

The familiar terror crashed over me. And as it started to pull me under, I heard a thought. But this thought was so loud that it felt like someone spoke it out loud. It came with such clarity that it grabbed me even in the middle of the fear. I couldn't shake that haunting voice. This had never happened before.

You will be a homosexual.

What? It came out of nowhere, and it made no sense. Could the devil make me gay? I didn't know, but there was such despair attached to those words. The despair didn't last, though. Just as quickly as the thought came, I felt a deep assurance welling up inside. This wasn't my future. This was a lie straight from hell.

I'd never encountered anything like this thought before. I was furious. Rage filled me, and I turned to bold, radical worship. I paced the living room floor singing out loud in the Spirit. The devil had crossed a line.

My worship grew wilder and more passionate, straight from my heart. In the middle of that song a new voice came, and it was louder than the lying voice. It carried the peace I knew, and though it wasn't audible, I knew God was speaking to me. It was a sovereign moment. "Psalm 116:3-9," He said.

I reached for my Bible on the coffee table and fumbled through the pages. I found the psalm and read it aloud:

The pains of death surrounded me,
And the pangs of Sheol laid hold of me;
I found trouble and sorrow.
Then I called upon the name of the Lord:
"O Lord, I implore You, deliver my soul!"
Gracious is the Lord, and righteous;
Yes, our God is merciful.
The Lord preserves the simple;
I was brought low, and He saved me.
Return to your rest, O my soul,
For the Lord has dealt bountifully with you.
For You have delivered my soul from death,
My eyes from tears,

And my feet from falling.
I will walk before the Lord
In the land of the living.

As I read those words, there was no denying that God had spoken directly to me, to my situation. I noticed how each verse spoke directly to what I was feeling.

When I first heard that demonic voice, I was overwhelmed with a feeling of hopelessness and the pains of death. But the psalmist had called on God in verse four just like I had, and God had showed mercy to him just as He had to me. God had brought peace and deliverance to me, just as He did the writer of that psalm. But this was the best part—through the psalm, God promised He would keep me safe. He gave me a promise about my destiny. I wasn't promised death. I would walk with God in the land of the living.

The power of God fell on me, and it overcame the hopelessness that had been crushing me only moments before. In an instant, the taunting voice was silenced, and the panic vanished. It was gone. I read the psalm again, and I knew God was speaking to me. I'd needed these verses, word for word, and it came like a knife, cutting through everything. And as I settled into the peace of His Word, I fell asleep.

I woke late the next morning and made my way to the kitchen. My dad was there, eating breakfast. He asked how the night had gone, expecting to hear it'd been a good night. I told him how crazy the night had been: there had been a demon sitting right next to me and he had told me I was going to be gay.

My dad asked why I hadn't come to get him. I told him I did just what he'd taught me to do. I'd gotten so angry and started to worship, and then I heard a louder voice say Psalm 116. I knew it was God. "As soon as I started reading, the fear was gone in a second. It was awesome!" I told him.

"This is a moment you'll never forget," he said. "Hold onto it."

That was an anchoring moment, filling me with confidence. What's more, it filled me with a promise, a tangible word from God I could read over and over again. I could declare it as a promise over my life when the fear came. No man or demon could take that moment or the truth of it from me. Before that night, I'd used verses my dad had found personal truth and freedom in, and that worked. But that night, Psalm 116 became mine. I'd fought and won my own personal battle. This passage wasn't a sword my dad had handed me. It was a sword that the Lord gave me and I personally picked up. I knew the power that it carried.

I'd received my own experience with God, and a person with an experience is never at the mercy of any argument, even if the argument is from the devil himself. Over the months and years that followed, I deepened that experience. With praise and worship the fear always broke. But as I got into high school, the normal teenage distractions set in, and a subtle shift started happening.

SIX

THE TWELVE STRING APPLAUSE

* * *

By my junior year of high school, things had changed. I still went to church and attended our church events, but other things now occupied me. Consumed by sports, I gave myself to basketball in the winter and baseball in the summer. I wanted to be the very best, and I became obsessed with working out every afternoon. I made the high school teams as soon as I could try out, and I started traveling throughout Northern California for games and tournaments. When I wasn't traveling for my own events, I went to Eric's baseball games and wrestling matches. We moved from one sports season to the next, and it became a distraction for me.

When I wasn't at the gym or playing sports, I found other things to distract me. I hung out with friends or spent time with my girlfriend. I grew further away from the reality of all that God had done in my life. As I did, my relationship with God became a bit shallow. And since everything in the life of the believer hinges on your personal relationship with God, I grew dull. And in that dullness, compromise crept into my life.

Some friends discovered a video tape with porn on it, and we watched it one night at a sleepover. It was my first real experience with porn, and after that moment, something awoke inside of me—a need. The pull toward porn grew. These were the days before smartphones and the Internet gave people easy access. My appetite for porn became more and more intense, and it seemed to grow even as I tried to fight it. The temptation, followed by my failure, became a discouragement.

The distraction of sports and my struggle with porn brought the same guilt I'd felt all those years ago when I was young, but this time I didn't let that guilt guide me to repentance. I'd compartmentalize the guilt that I felt. My heart wasn't hardened toward God, but the shame brought discouragement that this was a struggle. My Bible became more of a bedside prop than a place to find life and encouragement. I'd lost my focus, and it showed in the way I was living my life.

In this season of distraction, the panic was all but gone. I didn't experience the creeping fear that had so often been almost a constant companion. I usually slept through the night. It was a season of relative calm, and looking back, I know why. I wasn't moving forward in my relationship with God, and I grew lazy in my pursuit.

There are times we start down the wrong path, but even then, God finds a way to bring things around. I remember the day He intervened, though I didn't know it was a moment that would change the course of my life. Eric brought home an old Applause twelve-string guitar, and he'd removed the high strings and turned it into a six-string. For days, he played whatever chords he knew, and I thought it might be cool to learn a couple of chords so that I could play some songs with my youth pastor. I had Eric teach me just a couple of chords. One afternoon, while Eric was out, I walked over to that old Applause beside his bed, picked it up and strummed a chord.

In that moment the guitar became mine, and Eric never got it back.

I became obsessed with playing that guitar. I grabbed an old chord book and started teaching myself. When I wasn't at school or at practice, I was learning guitar. I couldn't put it down, and as I played, I found music

THE TWELVE STRING APPLAUSE   59

came naturally for me. What's more, I remembered how powerful worship was in my life. I began to feel that familiar pull to God again, so I played more and more worship music. I started writing a little, and as I did, my obsession with sports disappeared. I had my sights set on something new.

———————————————

The summer after my junior year of high school, I went with my youth group to Springs of Living Waters Camp in Chico, California. I didn't go with any expectations, but my expectations weren't needed for God to do something significant.

During a night session, God started moving. He felt close through worship, and then He spoke directly to me through the message. The preacher spoke about being consecrated to God, fully surrendering yourself to Him. As I listened, I knew my life had to change. I wasn't fully surrendered to God, and I felt the weight of conviction in my heart.

At the end of the message, the speaker invited us forward to rededicate our lives, and I knew I had to go forward. God was calling me into something more, so I didn't hesitate. I walked straight to the altar, and I knelt at the front. That was when everything came crashing down, and in that moment, I realized I was in the middle of a battle, because the anxiety and panic I hadn't felt in so long came rushing in. My heart pounded, and the fear of losing control was as strong as it had ever been. It was clear to me—this fear was directly related to the commitment I was about to make. Something was trying to keep me away from God, but I wouldn't give in. I said the prayer and surrendered everything as the fear grew stronger.

My small group leader, Andy Szolosi, was standing to my left, and I turned to him and told him I needed him to pray for me. I pulled some of my friends around me. I knew what I needed to do: I had to take charge in that moment. I had a history of battling this, and I knew that worship would bring breakthrough. My friends started singing with me. As we worshiped, the tears welled up in my eyes. The memories of God's faithfulness filled me, and I knew He'd be faithful again.

There, surrounded by a small group of friends, we worshiped. The terror was still pressing down, but it was as if our worship was a shield against it, and so we worshiped even harder, sang even louder. We were shameless, and I didn't care what anyone thought. The power of worship was working as heaven came close. Everything slowed as the weight of His Presence fell on us, and my fear and terror disappeared. It struck me—this was the first time I'd lead a group in worship.

I left camp that year with a new vision. I couldn't control the size of my life, but I could control the size of my worship. It was as if a line had been drawn in the sand and I stepped over it. As we made our way back to Weaverville, I was determined to live in complete surrender to God. I knew I couldn't be lazy or apathetic anymore. The days of casual living were over, and it was time to enter into a season of intense pursuit.

Back in Weaverville, I dedicated myself fully to God, and as I did, the Holy Spirit taught me some truths that before had just been nice thoughts: "Since we are receiving the rights to an unshakeable kingdom, we should be extremely thankful and offer God the purest worship that delights his heart as we lay down our lives in absolute surrender, filled with awe. For our God is a holy, devouring fire!" (Hebrews 12:28-29). As that became a reality in my life, I found God was consuming every idol. Things were different, and worship became my life. Writing music consumed the rest of my summer. I wrote a lot of songs, but none of them seemed to stick. Then I wrote "You're the Miracle of My Life." It was my first real song, and when I finished it, I decided to share it with my youth pastor. I wasn't sure what he would think.

The next day, I went straight to my youth pastor's office, Mike Morris. I told him about the song, and he asked me to play it for him.

"Brian, that's a good song," he said. "Would you play it at youth group this week?"

I'd never been asked to lead worship. I'd only played backup for Mike, and I'd never led worship in front of a group, but without even thinking about it, I said I'd do it.

That Wednesday night, Mike opened with worship, and I stood behind him, playing guitar. I focused as best I could on the chords and fought back the nerves. I'd be playing my song next, and I was sweating bullets by the time he strummed the last chord to the song he was leading.

It was finally my turn. I stepped up to the mic, strummed an A chord, and sang the first line, "You're the miracle of my life, and you set me free." As I played, all that nervous energy left as the crowd sang along. I knew in that moment that I was made for this. I had never felt more at home.

I stepped off the stage, and Linda Lee, a family friend, met me there.

"I feel like there's an anointing on your life for worship, and God has given you an authority for this" she said.

She'd only heard me play one song. How could she have had any idea about my future? But I knew she was right, and I held onto that prophetic word. It was a promise. It was the first time anyone had spoken a word over my life about worship.

I gave myself to that word, and after that service, I did anything and everything I could to grow as a worship leader. I practiced around the clock and led worship anytime and anyplace that I could. I started leading worship every week at a drug rehab group, and I led worship more regularly at youth group. I kept writing songs, mostly songs that came out of my own experience. Sometimes I pulled songs straight from the Bible and wrote them down on notecards so I could memorize them. By the end of the summer, all I wanted was to lead worship and write songs for the rest of my life.

I didn't see it in that moment, but God had used all those years of my childhood to prepare me to lead and write worship music. I knew I was supposed to write songs that connected people to the heart of God through pure and simple devotion because that kind of worship carries power and authority.

Through my experiences, I came to realize that when someone is healed instantly, it often speaks of their identity as a son or daughter of God. But when healing or freedom is progressive and takes place over time, it's often because that person is being trained for war, and when you're trained for war, you gain authority and power in that area. In those early years of panic, I was learning firsthand how praise and worship carry breakthrough and bring freedom. This understanding would be my cornerstone as I continued to write music.

The summer ended, and I entered my senior year of high school. The year before, I'd been obsessed with sports and working out. They were my idols, and so, as part of my surrender, I laid them down. I traded my preppy Zack Morris look for something different, growing a scraggly beard and letting my hair grow long. I bought some old jeans and tie-dyed shirts at a thrift store, changing everything about my style and look. And every day after school, instead of going to the gym, I went home, sat in my room and played guitar for hours. I never did anything halfway; I was always all in.

My choices weren't well received by everyone. In English class, a girl sitting next to me leaned over and asked what had happened to me. "You used to be so good looking," she said. "Now, you're so ugly." And though that kind of comment would have sent me spinning months earlier, in this new season of my life, it didn't even phase me. I had dedicated my life to God, and I didn't care what anyone thought.

During my senior year, I'd still come home after school each day and sit with my mom and talk about my day. After a few weeks of watching the changes in my life, she asked about the new look and quitting sports. Why had I dropped my old friends?

"This is what I'm supposed to do. I needed to make drastic changes to follow what God has for me," I said. "Don't worry, Mom."

"God has a plan in this," she said. "Since you were little, I've known God has called you to something special."

Years after the fact, I found out that when I came back from camp, my parents were nervous about my dramatic change. They weren't sure quitting sports and my new hippie look were the best choices. They didn't see the need for me to quit the gym either, though I knew I had to. But though they questioned my decisions, they didn't try to stop me. I continued to lead worship, and I found my own lane. I began to learn who I was in God without everything that used to define me. My parents gave me space, talked with me often, and kept praying for me. Pretty soon their concerns went away as they started to see the fruit of my life.

⏤⏤⏤⏤⏤⏤⏤

During the winter of my senior year, Bethel Church in Redding—the church where my grandpa had pastored so many years—called my dad. They needed a new senior pastor, and they wondered whether he'd be willing to come. He wasn't sure at first. He was happy at Mountain Chapel, and we were experiencing a move of God. So, without praying about it, he gave them an answer. He wouldn't leave Weaverville.

Only a few days later he heard from the Lord: "You didn't ask Me." My dad knew it was true. So my dad called Bethel Church and told them he'd interview for the position.

In those days, revival was in full swing in places like Brownsville and Toronto, and my parents had spent time at both. They'd experienced the Presence of God and miracles of those revivals firsthand. During the interview, my dad let the people at Bethel know he wanted to see revival come to Redding. If he became their pastor, he wouldn't change the subject. After the interview, they asked him to preach, and he preached about tithing, a topic that probably wasn't too popular. Still, the following week they offered him the position. He agreed to take the job, and in January 1996 my family said goodbye to Mountain Chapel.

We arrived in Redding, and revival broke out almost immediately. Things started happening. People were getting healed and set free, but it came with a cost. In those first few months, over a thousand people left the church, uncomfortable with what was happening. One person even said, "I know this is God, but it's just not for me." Still, my parents never changed the subject.

It was an exciting time at Bethel, and I was growing to love Redding. It was a bigger town, with more opportunities to lead worship, and with the move, school didn't take up so much of my day. I finished high school through independent study during the spring semester, having more time to practice my music, and that practice began to pay off. Scott Anderson, the youth pastor, invited me to join the staff as a youth intern, and he asked if I'd take over as the worship leader for the youth. I agreed without hesitating. It was exciting to get to build something from the ground up.

Every job, though, has its challenges, and being a youth intern in the 1990s was no exception. All I wanted was to lead worship, but as was the case with most youth groups in those days, our youth ministry didn't just have worship and a message. We also performed skits and played games, things I thought were pointless. I could handle the games but wanted absolutely nothing to do with the skits, and I certainly didn't try to hide my opinions. I told Scott and the rest of the staff I had no interest in participating in skits and games. I did whatever I could to avoid everything other than leading worship. I definitely pushed some buttons and wore a few people out. I didn't handle those conversations well, and it was a start to some of the communication problems that would follow me.

When I took over the youth worship team, I wanted everything we did to be excellent. I didn't want worship to be something that we simply checked off the list. I wanted excellent songs and high-quality sound. I knew that, combined with a heart for God, would connect people to Him.

I started looking for musicians who wanted to go after this with me. They'd need to understand we weren't just singing songs to fill the time before a message. They needed to be excellent on their instruments. They'd need to be able to improvise, too, because we were creating a space for God to move.

We were doing something new, and at first, some of the musicians didn't understand why it mattered. During one rehearsal, I confronted a musician who wasn't playing the right notes. He told me he wasn't able to focus on the notes and worship at the same time. I told him if he couldn't play the right chords, he could worship with the crowd. If he was going to be up on the stage helping lead worship, he needed to put the time in and learn the songs. We had a responsibility and couldn't be distracting. He didn't take it well. The situation was something that needed to be addressed, but I definitely could have said it better. The band kept improving, and as our youth worship team grew together, God did exactly what I imagined.

The worship experience in the youth group was gaining momentum, and we wanted to take it out into the community. So, a year into my internship, we decided to start a street ministry in downtown Redding. We would worship and evangelize, but it'd all be centered around the Presence of God. As we planned, we decided there'd be nights we'd only worship, and other nights we'd focus on reaching out to people.

Every Thursday night, Redding hosted a small fair with food and live music. Our band would gather on an empty corner, and people walking by would stop and listen. Afterward, they often struck up conversations. They could sense something different. What they didn't know was that they were experiencing the power of God through worship. The music seemed to open them up, and many of them came to know Jesus.

One night, a man walked right through the middle of our band, reached into his pocket and pulled out a bag of drugs. He threw them in the garbage can behind us and started to cry as he experienced God. No one had even talked to him; it was the atmosphere of worship that did something that caused him to be compelled to get rid of his drugs. This wasn't a one-off story though. Night after night, people gave their lives to Jesus.

Another Thursday night came, and a group of us met to worship. The street lights were shining in from either side of the street. While I played guitar, and we were worshiping, I looked to the left and saw a group of women approaching from one side of the street. They were normal-looking women, but the moment I saw them, I sensed a darkness, a heaviness. I told the team that we needed to really go after it.

The women circled us, and I felt an extreme heaviness close in around us. It was a presence that was not God. It felt like we were in the middle of a showdown, but I knew we were going to win. We were fighting a spiritual darkness and started singing louder.

After a few minutes, I started walking toward the women but kept worshiping, and as I did, the atmosphere started to change; we could all feel it. In that moment, the women turned around and left. Someone later told us

THE TWELVE STRING APPLAUSE

they were Wiccan. God had shown up in this battle between light and darkness, and there was no contest.

***

My theology of worship was formed through real-life experiences that were tested. The attacks of my youth were real-life issues that demanded real-life answers. I didn't need empty, powerless head knowledge. I needed experienced truth that grew from worshiping God, even in the pain, even in the darkness.

Jesus led a life of worship so connected with the Father that demons fled from His very Presence. His life of worship brought healing and deliverance. It pushed through the deepest pain of humanity and brought Him to the power of resurrection after death. It was that kind of worship that set people free, and as I began to chase after this kind of life, I not only experienced His healing and saving power, I was able to bring it to others.

But even though I'd experienced the Presence of God through worship, fifteen years later I was the one walking toward the back of an ambulance. I was the one who needed freedom.

I listened to the steady hiss of oxygen flowing from the tank as the EMTs told me to watch my head as I climbed in. They told Jenn she couldn't ride with us, and she followed us to the hospital. Even though the sedatives were working, there was still an overwhelming sense that something was really wrong. What was happening to me?

SEVEN

JENN ROCK

* * *

On a Friday afternoon in January 2004, my family watched as my grandpa suffered one of the most horrific and violent deaths from pancreatic cancer. In the years leading up to his passing, our family and our church had been praying for his healing. We'd been praying that our city would be a cancer-free zone. So, watching my grandpa suffer and lose his battle with the very thing we were praying against felt cruel.

No one took the loss harder than my dad. My grandpa was my dad's greatest supporter, and the pain was unimaginable. And though my dad had preached his core beliefs over the years—among which were the facts that God is good all the time and that sickness is from the devil—in the midst of such a devastating loss, it might have been easy for him to question God's goodness. It would have been easy for him to become bitter and offended. But he didn't.

Just two days after my grandpa's death, I watched as my dad spoke at Bethel and gave the most courageous message I'd ever heard, a message about his unshakable belief in the goodness of God. Through his tears, he spoke about the last few days we'd spent at my grandpa's bedside. He shared how we stood around my grandpa and told him how much we loved him. We had people with him around the clock, and over twenty of us worshiped for hours on end.

To watch the most horrible suffering you've ever seen and to rise above it and still give God praise was costly, but it was an honor to give that gift of worship.

"Anyone can be thankful when things are going well, but to give a gift of thanksgiving and praise in the middle of crisis is a true test," my dad said.

My dad shared how both he and my grandpa believed we were living in a time of great reformation, a time that would alter the course of history. They believed God would pour His Spirit out, that He'd bring healing to His people. My grandpa spent his life following that belief, working to bring that reformation to pass, even though he ultimately died at the hand of cancer. My dad shared how my grandpa's cruel, unjust and painful death at the hands of cancer wouldn't stop him. He would cry and mourn his father's loss. He would acknowledge the pain. But he would never allow that pain to derail him from going after revival and healing.

Often in the midst of great loss, people will reduce their theology to match their experience. My dad wouldn't allow the pain to draw him to wrong conclusions about the nature of God. Instead, he'd become even firmer in his belief, and he decided to choose faith. He asked all of us to make that decision, too. There was no other option; we had to believe even more in the goodness of God. We had suffered a loss, but now we were going to double our efforts as a church to go after the healing of cancer.

My dad ended his message with these words: "In heaven there won't be any pain, confusion or loss. So I embrace my moment of pain now and give Him praise in the midst of it. That's offering I'll never have a chance to give Him in heaven."

The closing words of my dad's message came back to me as I rode in the ambulance. I knew this moment of pain was an opportunity to give God an offering of worship. Under the weight of the fear and panic, I wanted to have the same courage I'd seen from my dad on that Sunday so many years ago. But choosing to worship under these circumstances wasn't easy. Though the sedative the EMT had given me at the house seemed to be working, the panic was still right there, pressing on my chest.

It was such a confined space in that ambulance, which didn't help my anxiety, and no matter how hard I tried, I couldn't take in a full breath on that twenty minute drive. I did my best to choose faith, even in the middle of all that fear. I sang under my breath. But more than asking God for something in that moment, I knew I needed to give Him something. This couldn't be an exchange where I worshiped Him so that He would give me peace. I needed to give an offering with no strings attached to it. I had to give what I had in that moment, which wasn't much.

I couldn't get a grip, but I also couldn't shake the truth of God's goodness. He would come. He always came. I just didn't know when. I held on to the truth that God wasn't causing this meltdown. He was the only one who could pull me out, and that's why I'd pulled Haley, Téa, and Braden close back at the house and told them, "This is when God becomes real."

The ambulance moved down the highway as the EMT worked. I looked around, seeing everything as if through a wide-angle lens. A clip was attached to my finger to monitor my pulse. A wire ran up from it to a beeping machine. I had a mask over my nose and mouth with oxygen flowing through it, and an IV pumped something into my veins.

The drugs were finally kicking in because my heart rate felt like it was slowing even more. It wasn't jumping out of my chest. I pressed the mask down to make sure the seal was tight and took the deepest breath I could. It wasn't a full breath, but it was the best breath I'd had in hours. If a little sedative was good, if it could slow things down and help me breathe, then a little more would be better. I asked the EMT what he had given me at the house.

He told me the name of the drug, then asked if it was working. I nodded and asked, "Can I have more?"

He didn't answer me, but he reached for a syringe and pumped another dose into my IV. If the first shot of that sedative had helped me get a grip, this dose brought a thick numbness, and I closed my eyes as the harsh lights in the ambulance seemed to dim. The pressure in my chest released, and everything seemed to dull. Conversations from the hours before came back to me, like how the EMTs told Jenn this wasn't a heart attack, at least, not as far as they could tell. It looked more like a panic attack, they said.

The ambulance came to a stop, and the doors opened. A nurse waited with a wheelchair, and the EMTs helped me out as they gave the nurse the rundown. "We think it's a panic attack," one of them said. I heard it all, even though it was strangely muffled. The nurse nodded before wheeling me through the waiting area and into a small, curtained-off room. She helped me from the chair and into the bed.

There was a blur of movement outside my curtain walls, but I was numb to all of the activity around me. Doctors talked with patients, nurses whispered and machines beeped. The lights were even brighter there than they had been in the ambulance, if that was possible. The skin of my forearm pinched under the tape of my IV. Less than an hour ago, this much sensory input would have been more than I could handle, but now, everything was strangely muted.

It seemed like an eternity before Jenn walked through the curtain, and when I saw her, I broke into tears. It was a slow, deep sob, and for the life of me, I couldn't stop it. Crying? This wasn't me. It's not that I never cried, but I'd never experienced this surge of uncontrollable emotion. I was an artist, sure, but I wasn't the sort who lived from his feelings. Yet there I was, falling apart.

One hour passed. Then another. Jenn and I sat behind the curtain alone and held hands. The reality of what had happened set in. I had completely lost it, and though I knew God would show up and break through somehow, I wondered, *Will I ever be the same?*

A doctor walked in, introduced himself and asked me a few questions. I answered the questions as best I could. "The fear came out of nowhere," I told him. "No matter how hard I tried, I couldn't shake it. Overwhelming wasn't the right word," I said. "It was tormenting."

He repeated the EMT's question. Had I been under a great deal of stress?

Had I been under an unusual amount of stress? "Uhhh . . . yes," Jenn said. "That's an understatement. A crazy amount of stress and pressure. For a long time. It's been building for years, and this summer it has snowballed."

The doctor nodded along and said, "Your body might be showing you your limits. There is only so much stress and tension you can fill your body with. There comes a point where the brain can't handle any more, and everything just sort of shuts down."

Stress had been building for years. I could have told him about our never-ending house remodel, a remodel that was significantly over budget and way behind schedule, already a four-year project. I could have told him about the mismanagement of my financial advisor, how the implications were overwhelming. I could have told him of the issues that came with starting and growing Bethel Music. I could have told him about the struggles of being part of a church that had become a major movement.

To add to all this, I couldn't turn it off when I got home. I replayed every source of stress in my mind on an endless loop, and it was affecting my relationship with my wife and kids. And as hard as it was on the kids, it was even harder on Jenn. We were constantly talking through some source of stress in our life. The combination of balancing a family, a business, touring, ministry, and the church was too much. Even thinking about it exhausted me. And though I could have shared these things with the doctor, I didn't. Instead, I just laid there, quiet.

His question exposed a truth hidden in plain sight. I'd been so busy that I hadn't stopped to consider the combined weight of the stress, pressure and conflict. And even if I did, it wasn't anything I could just quit. Even with the difficulties, I loved what I was a part of building. We could've done less, but we felt like we were doing what God had called us to do.

But the things we were involved in weren't the problem. Over the years, I'd taken the negative emotion, every frustration and hurt, and I'd pushed it down, thinking if I ignored it, it would all go away. It didn't. All those undealt-with emotions had finally caught up with me.

The doctor interrupted my thoughts, and he asked if I'd experienced this sort of panic before. Jenn told him I'd experienced something similar as a child, but it had never been this bad. The doctor listened and nodded. He turned to me and asked for the specifics. I told him about my childhood but said this felt different. As a kid, the terror felt more spiritual, but this was more physical. I didn't know if he understood me, if he had the framework to understand the difference between the two, but the sedatives had loosened my ability to care, so I talked freely.

The doctor thought I'd had a major anxiety attack, a nervous breakdown really. The shortness of breath, the rapid heartbeat, the sensory overload—these were common symptoms of stress and anxiety, and my body was trying to tell me I was overloaded. "Something had to give," he said, "and in the end that something was you." He told me I'd need to stay a few more hours for observation, just to make sure there weren't any irregularities, but I could go home at the end of the night.

He walked out the way he'd come in through the Emergency Room hallway. Jenn held my hand as I closed my eyes. I was so tired, completely worn out.

"You're going to be okay," she said. "We'll figure this out together. We'll make it through."

I asked Jenn how the kids were, and she said they'd been really freaked out, but they were okay. She'd left them with my mom and dad, but after my parents calmed them down, they'd loaded up the car and come to the hospital. On cue, Haley, Téa, Braden and my parents came through the curtain. I don't remember what I said, if anything. I don't remember much, but I remember them being there, and somehow that was enough.

I looked at Jenn and remembered when I had experienced that final breakthrough all those years ago just before we were married. We'd thought it was finished, thought I was done with panic in my life. But for some reason, here I was again, and I felt for Jenn. When you say for better or worse, sickness and health, you mean it. And now, Jenn had been thrown right in the middle of the worse.

I remember those early days of leading worship at Bethel, how exciting it was. God was showing up and doing incredible things. I stepped onto the stage to lead worship for the Sunday night service, and as I turned to the crowd, I saw her standing near the center aisle. She was wearing cutoff jean shorts and a red T-shirt. I recognized her immediately.

Jenn Rock.

Jenn was my younger sister's age. She had lived on the coast, a few hours away from Redding, but she and Leah had known each other for years.

They'd been camp friends since the sixth grade. But Jenn wasn't in sixth grade anymore. She was seventeen and had graduated from high school early. And let me tell you, there was a big difference between the girl I knew as my little sister's friend, and the girl standing in the crowd that night.

When I saw her, I lost my focus. She threw any thought of leading worship right out the window. I had one thing on my mind: how could I impress her? I kept hoping it was the best set I'd ever led and that I'd appear extra anointed as I played. I kept looking in her direction, but our eyes never met. She was focused on worship, and she didn't seem to notice me at all.

I tried my best to finish the worship set undistracted, but when I stepped off the stage, I went straight to Gabe, the keyboard player who would become my sister's future husband. He was known as a matchmaker back in those days, so I told him he had to connect me with Jenn. He told me he'd make it happen.

I talked to Leah that night hoping to get some more information. She said Jenn and her family had just moved to Redding from Humboldt County, California. They'd sold everything so that Jenn and her parents could attend the Bethel School of Supernatural Ministry. Now that Jenn lived in Redding, she and Leah were spending a lot of time together. If I wanted, Leah could make sure we connected. I smiled and said I wouldn't stop her.

I walked into the church administration office the next day, and I spotted Gabe in the workroom. He was talking to Jenn, so instead of walking by as I might have on any other day, I made a detour to stop and talk. She was sweet and friendly, but she showed no interest. And though she'd tell me years later that she'd had a crush on me since she was twelve, I never would have known it that day. She was playing hard to get, and if I wanted a relationship with Jenn, I was going to have to work for it.

In those days, after any service, a group of us would go to Denny's or Black Bear Diner, the only places in Redding open after our church got out in the evening. I was more of an introvert and couldn't have cared less about hanging out with the group after church, but I wanted to be around Jenn, so I always went and made sure to sit near her. For two months, that was our rhythm. She gave me just enough to keep me on the hook but not enough to know whether she wanted something more than friendship.

Even though she seemed to be at every meeting and service I was at, she'd often exit a room when I walked in. But as time went on, I started to figure her out. I could tell she was into me, but she was going to make me work for this. I'd never had that before, and I liked it.

By the end of the summer, we still weren't spending time together alone, but our group became smaller. There were four of us who spent most of our time together—me, a guy friend of ours, Jenn and a friend of hers. And though I'd tried to get the group down to two—Jenn and me—it was all but impossible to get that girl alone. And even if she would have agreed to spend time with me alone, my friend was making it difficult.

One Thursday night we dropped the girls off at Jenn's house and made our way back to the church to pick up my car. My friend turned to me, out of the blue, and told me that Jenn didn't like me. In fact, Jenn liked him, he said. That's when he "explained" the situation to me. "Jenn is the kind of girl you have to take your time with," he said. He laid out his detailed plan for reeling her in. I listened without saying a word, although I was trying hard not to laugh. When he finished, he dropped me off at my car, and I made a decision. There was no way I was going to sit back and watch this clown pursue Jenn. It was time to let her know how I felt.

I was outside the church the next day when I saw Jenn leaving the prayer chapel alone. This was my moment. I caught up with her and asked her if we could meet in my office. She agreed, followed me in, and we sat down. I said everything you're not supposed to say. I told her I liked her and that she had all the qualities I wanted in a wife. I really opened up and went for it. To my surprise, she told me she'd just been in the prayer chapel asking God to either take away her feelings for me or make it clear that we were supposed to be married. We looked at each other and laughed. "So we're together?" I asked. And just like that, we were. It might seem rushed, and I certainly wouldn't recommend this to most, but it was right. And to this day, we don't have a single regret.

We didn't waste any time, and within two days, we both knew. We were getting married. And sure, looking back now I can see how fast it was, but it didn't feel fast in the moment. It just felt right.

Four days into dating, I went to talk to my dad. I told him Jenn was the one for me, and I wanted to marry her. I asked him what he thought. My parents had known Jenn since she was a little girl. They loved her. He looked at me, smiled, and said, "Brian, she's the one. Marry that girl." I had his blessing.

That night, we led worship together for the first time. It was crazy how comfortable it felt, and after the service we talked about it. We knew we were made to do this together. After the service, we went back to my parents' house. We were all in the living room when a close family friend showed up at the house. She had called my mom earlier that week and asked if I was dating anyone. My mom laughed and said, "Why, yes, he is!" I guess it confirmed something, because there she was at the door, asking my dad if she could speak to Jenn and me.

She had a word and a vision for us, and she asked if she could come share it and pray over us. My parents recorded the prayer on a cassette tape. She prophesied that we had an anointing for worship. We would write songs for the church and start a worldwide worship movement. She said she saw God putting us together like a whirlwind, but we would know it was Him because of the great peace we would have. After she gave us the word, she prayed over us. The Presence of God was felt by everyone in that room. It was the first word we received as a couple, and God showed up as if to affirm it all. It was incredible.

Five days into our relationship, I asked Jenn's parents, Ron and Sandra Rock, to dinner. We met at an Outback Steakhouse—a nice place for a twenty-year-old with no money—and I sat across from Jenn's parents. I barely knew them and was uncomfortable, so I got straight to the point. I asked them for their permission to marry Jenn. What was an already awkward moment was made even more awkward by the fact that the waitress appeared just after I asked the question. She put two small loaves of bread on the table, took our drink orders, and made her way back to the kitchen, oblivious that she'd interrupted the most important question of my life. I waited for some word from them, but they didn't answer my question. Instead, Ron asked me to tell him the things I liked about his daughter—All Of The Things.

Was he serious?

It felt like an impossible question, and I couldn't even think straight, I was so nervous. I don't remember what I said, but I remember this: my hands were sweating, my stomach was turning, and within just a couple of minutes, I ate both loaves of bread. Whatever I said must have convinced Ron because he started laughing, then gave me his permission, even though we'd only been together a few days.

Six days in, I went to my mom. I told her I had a little money but it wasn't enough for a ring. She gave me the rest, and I went to a local jeweler to find a ring. I found the perfect ring, a diamond in a simple gold band. It only cost seven hundred dollars and wasn't much, but it was enough. It was perfect.

I had my ring, and I had a plan. It was the next Sunday evening, and Jenn was playing keys and leading worship with me. I stepped up to the microphone and prayed a short prayer that ended with an "Amen." Then I turned to Jenn and said, "Oh, and one more thing. Will you marry me?" The crowd went wild cheering. Jenn didn't see this coming at all! She nodded and walked toward me. I put the ring on her finger, and the crowd cheered again.

We prayed and talked to our parents about when to get married. We all agreed that spring break would be perfect, which was in about seven months. Shortly after that I started my second year of school of ministry, and Jenn started her first year. During our engagement, we spent most of our time in school, traveling, doing street ministry and leading worship together.

It was obvious to anyone who heard her sing that Jenn had an undeniable gift. She carried authority in her voice, and her ability to flow in spontaneous worship was powerful. And time after time, as we finished leading worship, people came to us with prophetic words, and those words were always so similar to the word we were given before we got engaged.

It was such a good season, but I continued to struggle with fear. And when I did, I didn't hide it from Jenn. She didn't think twice when it would flare up and would help me pray through it. She was all in.

Just a couple of weeks before our wedding, I boarded a small regional plane with my mom, headed to Los Angeles to lead worship. It was only a one-hour flight, and I hadn't had a panic attack for months, though in the weeks leading up to that trip, I'd been more and more nervous knowing I was going on a small plane. As I stepped on the plane, the claustrophobia set in. I pushed it back and convinced myself I'd be fine.

I made my way down the aisle, and as I did, I looked out the window. That's when I noticed I wasn't on a jet. This was a prop plane, and somehow that made the claustrophobia worse. As I walked down that very long aisle to our seats at the very back of the plane, I could feel the familiar shift in the air.

As we got to our row, my mom took the window seat.

I slid into the aisle.

I felt the pressure around me start to build even more.

The attendant moved to the front of the plane and closed the door as the props of the plane spun up. The weight on my chest started to press in. The panic increased as the plane pulled away from the airport and made its way to the runway. We gained speed, and the cabin pressure seemed to push down on me. I grabbed the seat arms as we started to lift off the ground. I was trapped in this plane for the next hour, and I rocked back and forth, trying to keep it together as we were about to climb to twenty thousand feet.

Wide-eyed, I leaned over to my mom and told her I was freaking out. I didn't have to say much. She'd seen this look of terror on my face before, so she handed me her Bible and opened it up to Psalm 91. I knew this psalm but also knew it wasn't what I needed. I needed a psalm of praise to get me through. I flipped to Psalm 150 and began reading it out loud.

> Praise the Lord!
> Praise God in His sanctuary;
> praise Him in His mighty firmament!
> Praise Him for His mighty acts;
> praise Him according to His excellent greatness!
> Praise Him with the sound of the trumpet;
> praise Him with the lute and harp!
> Praise Him with the timbrel and dance;
> praise Him with the stringed instruments and flutes!
> Praise Him with loud cymbals;
> praise Him with clashing cymbals!
> Let everything that has breath praise the Lord.
> Praise the Lord!

I read the psalm over and over, but reading wasn't enough. The anxiety kept building and growing stronger. So, I started to sing quietly. I sang the words of that psalm to some made-up tune in my head. I sang them over and over again. People started looking at me, but I didn't care. I just kept singing.

Nothing seemed to change. I'd never been this far gone in a panic attack, especially in public. I sang with more intensity, and if the lady to my right thought I was crazy before, she was likely convinced of it now. I kept carrying on anyway. Ten minutes passed, then twenty, and I was beside myself. I felt like I might pass out, which would have been a gift if it meant escaping the torment.

For thirty minutes I sang that psalm with a combination of desperation and faith, fighting for peace. Then the fear and anxiety vanished in an instant. Gone. The air was normal and filled with peace. That's when I heard God give me a promise that went right into my soul.

I've given you the keys to freedom and you are going to bring that freedom to those who are locked in the same sort of fear.

It wasn't an audible voice. It was quiet, a deep knowing. I was more sure of it than anything, and in that moment, I knew I was at the end of a fifteen-year chapter of my life. I'd never suffer from this kind of torment again.

I didn't have another panic attack after that, at least not until I ended up in that hospital bed, fifteen years later. But I knew something significant happens when we choose praise in the moments of our greatest struggle and pain. I'd experienced it firsthand.

EIGHT

LIVING IN THE MATRIX

* * *

There are times to shield your kids and protect them, but I knew this wasn't one of those times. They watched me spiral into panic. They saw me lying in the hospital bed, the medicine making me numb. I wanted them to see the reality of my pain. I knew shielding them would be more detrimental than beneficial. I wanted them to see my desperation so that when I got through this, they would see how faithful God had been.

The kids stood around my hospital bed, silent and staring. The doctor came and told us that I needed to take it easy, that I needed to take a break. I was going to need some help getting over this. He handed a slip of paper to Jenn, explaining that it was a prescription for a sedative that would help get me through this and help me stay on top of my anxiety while I healed.

"It's the same sort of drug that's running through his IV right now," he said.

I held Jenn's hand as she walked me through the waiting area, out the double doors and toward the car. The tightness and anxiety were mostly gone. It wasn't the same kind of peace I'd experienced as a child—this was a medical peace—but even still, I didn't care. This medicine felt like some kind of miracle. I fell asleep as soon as I got home and slept through the night.

I woke the next morning into a new reality. The anxiety had returned, though it wasn't as pressing. My mind felt fragile. I was on edge, and at any moment, I might fall apart like I had the night before. I crawled out of bed, made my way to the kitchen and took my morning pill. I bent over the kitchen counter and waited for it to kick in. I was grateful I didn't have anywhere to be. We'd just wrapped up our two-week school of worship with students from around the world. And knowing that, Jenn and I had already blocked out the upcoming week for vacation. We had planned to use the time to rest and hang out with our kids after that busy two weeks, having no idea I would now need it to recuperate from a breakdown.

Jenn came into the kitchen to check on me. She'd called our family doctor, and we had an appointment in an hour. The sedatives were finally working, and my breathing evened out. I went to the bedroom, got dressed and the two of us made our way to the doctor's office.

I told him what had happened. He said I should consider counseling and said I definitely needed to make some lifestyle changes. I needed to slow down, take some time off and find things to cut from my life. I should consider eliminating sugar, caffeine and any other stimulants that might add anxiety in my body.

"You need to do everything you can to create peace and calm in your life," he said. Jenn told him we'd scheduled a couple of weeks off: he smiled and said that was a good start. He said that I should prepare myself, though. I would need more than a couple of weeks.

I committed myself to rest during that first week, and I didn't leave the house. I spent my time on the couch or in bed, and I didn't even open my computer. I played worship music through the house speakers most of the day and through the night. Before this all started, I had been writing a song with my friend Jason Ingram, who I have to say is one of the greatest worship songwriters of our time. I played that song, "Greater Than All Other Names," over and over again. It was a simple recording, a demo version of Jason singing while playing an old piano.

> *"Your love outlasts the deepest pain. Your arms still reach the furthest place. Your light still shines to light up the darkest night. Though waters rise beyond the shore. Though mountains fall, still I am yours. Your name is still great. Much greater than all other names.*
>
> *You are more than enough. You are mighty to save. You are all that you said you would be. You have already won. You laid death in the grave. Through the power of the cross I am free."*

There was something special about this simple recording. I put this song on repeat, and it brought me an undeniable peace.

I slept nearly fifteen hours a day and had no energy. When I was awake, I knew exactly when I could take the next pill. When the meds hit my system, everything relaxed, and my body calmed. I rode the waves of those chemical highs and lows, and in those lows, I was shaky. But with another pill, I could make it through another few hours. I stayed on the couch for the first week, dazed. As I rolled into the second week, I became more aware of my surroundings, and that's when it became clear: even with the meds, I was not thinking the way I used to. My mind now seemed to experience normal situations in a completely new way.

I looked out the window at our backyard. Our lawn maintenance guy had come, and he'd missed a patch of grass. I focused on it. It absolutely drove me nuts. I needed him to take care of it immediately. I couldn't handle it.

I turned back toward the kitchen. It was clean for the most part, but someone had left a glass out. Why was I so bothered by it?

A new strange compulsion toward perfection had set in, and the slightest flaw or oversight was exaggerated in my mind. But it wasn't just disorder that bothered me. The kids playing loudly, the lawn mower, construction sounds—any noise was too much. When I left the house, I usually wore earplugs to quiet the noise. Everything felt chaotic, and in that chaos, my anxiety would stir up.

The second week passed, and though things weren't back to normal, I wanted to get back to work, but Jenn didn't think it was a good idea. She asked if I would take some more time off because she knew I wasn't ready. I didn't think I could, I said. Our schedule was getting busier than ever. There were meetings I was missing, and Jenn and I had upcoming events and tours to plan. There were songs in production and post-production at Bethel Music. There was too much to do.

"I'll take it easy," I promised. "I'll ease back into work. I'll be fine."

Jenn listened, and when I finished talking, she asked if I thought it was the best idea. She shook her head. "You always promise it'll be okay, Brian," she said, knowing my history, "but once you go back in, work will take over."

I should have listened. I didn't.

The following day, I was in the office trying my best to keep it low-key. By midday, I was overwhelmed. Everything that was on my list felt impossible. Each task seemed to take all my energy, and I couldn't seem to do even the smallest thing without intense concentration. What would have been a quick decision before now required all of my focus. Even a simple conversation with a musician about something so small I can't recall what it was, seemed like a huge disagreement. Whatever coping skills I'd had before my break were gone.

We were working through some minor problems, but now everything felt major. I couldn't differentiate between big and small issues anymore. Something was clearly different, and I was living in a completely new reality.

After work, I came home to the normal busyness of family life with three kids—usually more than three because they had their friends over all the time. There were things to do around the house, and I needed to spend time with the kids and Jenn, but all of it was too much. What had been my normal life now felt overwhelming. If the kids started to get loud, I'd just walk out of the house and go for a walk, leaving Jenn to be both mom and dad.

As the weeks passed, I stuck to my schedule and took my medicine without fail. I was consumed with making sure the anxiety didn't come back, but it was always right there; I could feel it right on the edge of any place. Managing my anxiety was a full-time job, and I had no emotional space anymore. Even though I cared for Jenn and the kids more than anything, I was incapable of thinking about their needs. I was completely exhausted.

Looking back, I see how life became all about managing my anxiety. I took my meds religiously, and if the panic didn't take me out, it was a good day. For that first month, the medicine worked for me. What I couldn't see, though, was that it was just a band-aid. It was helping me survive, and for a while it helped me feel like I was getting better. As the days passed, though, it seemed to take more and more to manage my day-to-day stress, and the minute I tried to jump back into normal life, I couldn't cope.

I'd find out later that long-term that medicine can exaggerate panic and anxiety. In order to get rid of the anxiety, you have to deal with the underlying cause. But the fact was, I didn't know what the underlying issue was or how it was affecting me.

⸺⸺⸺⸺⸺⸺⸺⸺

About six weeks after my breakdown, my daughter Téa invited a few friends to the house for a camp-out. I was in the backyard, setting up a couple of tents. I knew how hard this had been on the kids over the past couple of months, and I wanted her to do something fun. Téa had been so excited about inviting her friends over, and I wanted to give her a great night. She'd been such a champ these past couple of months. She's the life of the party and just needed to have some fun with her friends.

The girls were there, talking and laughing like girls do, and I could feel the pressure building. I started a fire so the girls could make s'mores, and as I sat by that fire, the pressure continued to build. Jenn sat next to me, and asked if I was okay. "I'm slipping," I said, but how could I explain it?

I was questioning the reality of the world around me, and overwhelmed by the possibility that my entire life was fake, that I was in a Matrix-like reality and was about to wake up and discover everything I thought to be true was a lie. I'd never had doubts like this before, so I repeated the truth over and over again in my mind:

The world is real,
This moment is real,
God is real,
He is good,
I'm okay,
I'm not going crazy.

It felt like my mind was slipping into a blackhole of insanity. The weight of unbelief and hopelessness was unimaginable.

The girls kept laughing and talking, unaware of my inner turmoil. And even though I knew these thoughts weren't true, I couldn't reason them away. In that moment, I didn't know what to believe.

The pressure settled heavier on my chest, and I took a deep breath. I couldn't keep my head above water. I leaned over to Jenn. "I feel like I'm actually going insane," I said. She stopped me and told me to look her in the eyes. Over and over she told me, "You're going to be okay. You're going to be okay." Her words helped me find a small sense of reality to hold on to.

I went in the house to take my medication. It was a desperate moment, so I didn't just take one. I took an extra pill, hoping to find more immediate relief. After twenty minutes, the mental numbness finally settled in. When it came, I convinced myself that I was getting better, even if it took an extra pill to drive the panic away.

It was October, a couple of months into my breakdown, and I was in a meeting for Bethel Music. A ball had been dropped, and it wasn't a small one. The team was frustrated. They were scrambling, trying to figure out what to do. There were so many opinions and a lot of disagreement on how we should move forward. I could feel my chest start to burn. If I ignored it, maybe this panic attack wouldn't come. After all, it hadn't been that long since I'd taken my last pill. I should be fine. I pressed my hand to my chest, trying to take a deeper breath.

As the tension in the room grew, so did my anxiety. I sat there as long as I could, but I couldn't handle it anymore. I was overwhelmed with the feeling that I wanted to quit. I just wanted to be done.

I stood from the table without a word and walked to the door, trying to get out of the room as fast as I could. I walked through the conference-room door and ran to my truck. It was happening all over again, and I had to get home. The anxiety got intense quickly, and I knew it was a bad one—one that might send me to the hospital if I didn't get on top of it. I couldn't go back there. I'd do anything to keep myself from spiraling like that again.

Within minutes, I was pulling into my driveway. I ran through the door into the kitchen, reached for the pill bottle, poured two in my hand and reached for another bottle. I'd periodically have to take a painkiller for neck pain, a problem that had developed years before. I poured one of those painkillers in my hand, opened the fridge, grabbed a beer, and washed all the medicine down.

Nothing changed, and the panic was unrelenting, so I grabbed another beer and drank it. I waited for the buzz as I sat at the kitchen table.

Should I quit everything?

I wanted to crawl into a hole and be done, to remove myself from anything that could even cause me anxiety and fall into a state of permanent numbness. I closed my eyes, and when I did the combination of what I took finally started to kick in to my system. Everything mellowed.

That's when the reality of the last thirty minutes came crashing in. I thought I'd been getting better, but clearly I wasn't. Without my pills, I couldn't function. I was only treating the symptoms of my breakdown, but there were some underlying problems I clearly hadn't dealt with. And in that moment, I made a decision:

This cannot be my future.

What just happened cannot happen again.

I will figure this out and deal with whatever the problem is.

This will not be my future.

A mental breakdown doesn't happen overnight, but in that moment, I couldn't see how everything had led me to my breakdown. There'd been a slow building of pressure over the years. Focused as I was, and great at stuffing my emotions, I had missed it.

Our first year of marriage was a breeze. Jenn and I lived in a one-bedroom apartment in Redding. I worked at the church, and Jenn taught piano lessons at our house. We never fought, not even over the things newlyweds typically disagree about. Things seemed simple, even easy. We were so happy.

During that first year, my dad gave Jenn and me leadership over the worship team at Bethel Church. Jenn and I were full of vision. We had received prophetic word after prophetic word about what we were called to do. We wanted to build a bridge between two great worship movements—the movement known for writing the songs the global church was singing, and the group known for its prophetic worship. We wanted a strong local worship community, not just people who played on a Sunday together, but a family—a big family. Jenn and I took the reins, and we didn't waste any time. We knew this was God's heart.

The worship at the church had always been strong in the prophetic. But now we wanted to marry the excellence of song and musicianship with the strength of the prophetic edge. We weren't dialed and polished, but we were passionate. We learned to communicate and improvise, but it was messy.

Months passed and our vision didn't fully match what was actually happening. I'd known from the beginning it'd take time to realize that vision, but it was taking more time than I'd imagined. There were disagreements over style, song choice and sound. It was frustrating and messy, not what I was envisioning, but God was still moving.

To make things more complicated, some of the people on the worship team had been friends of the family for years and had known me since I was a kid. Some couldn't seem to make the transition to seeing me in a leadership role, especially those who had known me as a baby. It was hard for some to make the transition to the new sound and others didn't think the financial investment into worship made sense, especially with all the other things the church could spend their money on. And I definitely didn't fit in as a typical pastor. All of these things, combined with my avoidance for confrontation, was a recipe for complications to come in.

This is where I need to own some of the mistakes I made. As time went on, Jenn and I met with many of the team about improving their skills by getting voice lessons or working on their instrument. Confrontation wasn't my strong suit, so I didn't tell the musicians why some things just weren't working. I didn't realize I wasn't being clear in my communication, and some of the team were making assumptions about what was happening. If people have no information, they will naturally fill in the gaps of the story. I wasn't giving them all the information, so they naturally came to their own conclusions.

Jenn and I were also leading the youth worship. I brought up some new musicians from the youth group to join the worship team, most of them really young, just thirteen to fifteen years old. We always tried to raise up young worship leaders and musicians, but I didn't communicate why. I left too much space for the team to make assumptions, including the assumption that they were being replaced. It didn't occur to me to reassure the veteran musicians and better communicate the vision for where we were going, so naturally misunderstandings happened. We were changing a lot of things, and change is difficult for anyone.

As the misunderstandings grew, so did my frustration, but I wasn't willing to talk about it, at least not with those I needed to. Instead, I just hoped everyone would catch the vision. I'd already shared it once. Wasn't that enough? Why couldn't they see what we were doing and where we were going? I didn't understand why I kept coming up against so much resistance. I hadn't yet learned that a vision has to first be communicated, then communicated again, then again. I hadn't learned that leaders overcommunicate to give everyone an opportunity to understand where things are going.

It was an unrealistic expectation—the expectation that they'd catch on without more coaching—and unrealistic expectations always lead to disconnection. I wouldn't try to understand their perspective. Instead, I kept pushing ahead, and it did not serve me well. God was moving, but it was painful for myself and others.

———

Don Potter visited during that season to lead worship for a Bethel conference. He was part of a nationwide ministry, and he was respected for his prophetic insight and excellence in music. On the last night of his visit, he called Jenn and me to the stage on a Sunday night. He laid hands on us and prayed over us in front of the entire church. It was a commissioning. Don affirmed our vision for this next season of ministry, and it filled me with renewed purpose. And then Don prayed over us; he said that I carried the same mantle for worship that my grandpa had.

My grandpa had been the senior pastor at Bethel Church for thirteen years, and he paid a heavy price to make worship a priority. He showed the church that worship wasn't just singing a song. It was a heart posture of surrender. It'd been foreign in those days, but my grandpa wasn't willing to change the conversation, and eventually it led to huge disagreements in the church. He was willing to be misunderstood for the congregation to experience the power of authentic worship. In the years that followed, Bethel Church experienced so much freedom in worship, in large part because of my grandpa's sacrifice. He'd been willing to fight for something, and it changed everything.

I was willing to fight for something too. I knew it when I heard Don's word. Jenn and I would keep moving forward, even if the team didn't understand. And that's exactly what happened. I knew worship changed everything, knew it firsthand, and wanted others to experience that same freedom.

Sometimes, uncomfortable things were said, and I felt misunderstood. But I'd always been good at ignoring my pain, and that's just what I did. I didn't deal with my frustration. I convinced myself I was fine. I told myself that where we were headed, not everyone would go. While that was true, I was also avoiding the frustration and hurt that I was feeling in the process.

So many of these things are a natural part of rapid growth in an organization. I know that. We doubled our staff multiple times in a short amount of time, and communication became even more complicated. The growth in staff, the competition for resources, and my lack of communication were a ticking time bomb for my internal world.

Although our ministry life was full of challenges, Jenn and I were great. We loved being married. We bought our first house with the help of Jenn's parents eight months after we were married. It was a great little first house that we loved fixing up and making a home.

Just a few months later we were out of town on our one-year anniversary. Jenn woke up not feeling well. The next morning she didn't feel well again. "What if I'm pregnant?" Jenn said with a massive smile on her face. We were so excited as we drove to get a test. Sure enough we were pregnant! We called our families, not able to wait to tell them the good news.

While Jenn was pregnant, we continued to travel and lead worship as well as write songs. We were at a leaders conference, and we were approached by a man named Andrew Sievright. He said what we were doing was really special, and he wanted to help us record an album of the songs we'd written. He would cover the costs and allow us to use his recording studio. We couldn't believe it! Our dream of recording an album was about to happen! Recording an album became another layer to an already busy life, but we couldn't have been more excited.

On December 11, 2001, Jenn went into labor. She wanted to labor as much as possible walking outside before going to the hospital. After a few hours, Jenn said she didn't feel well, like she had the flu. This was our first baby, and she didn't fully know what to expect with labor. Neither did I. When we got to the hospital, they admitted her and began the monitoring process. Within minutes, five nurses surrounded the hospital bed. They didn't say much, just shuffled in and out. We had no idea if this was normal. Then one of the nurses called the doctor. "The baby's vital signs are plummeting," she said.

The doctor gave the order, and the nurse turned to me, said Jenn needed to be rushed to the operating room for an emergency C-section. She unlocked the wheels, pushed the bed away from the wall and out the door without saying a word. I called my parents and her parents and told them to come. I followed the nurse to the surgical room door, but they wouldn't let me in as they prepped her for surgery. I was a mess. I sat out in the hall with my whole world on the other side of that operating room door.

Our family got there and sat with me, praying. When they were ready for surgery, they opened the door and brought me in. She was lying on her back with a surgical sheet blocking us from seeing below her neck. I sat down by her as they started the surgery. I felt like passing out, but I tried to be strong for Jenn. It felt like an eternity but was actually about thirty minutes. And then I heard it. Our little girl, Haley Bren, cried for the first time. It was one of the sweetest sounds I had ever heard.

They cleaned her up and took her vitals. She had very low numbers, so a nurse brought her over to us so we could see her but then told us they had to take her to the NICU. She rushed out of the operating room with our tiny baby girl in her arms. After the doctors finished the surgery, we were taken back to a hospital room to recover. A NICU doctor came in and told us that Haley had an APGAR score of two out of ten. He said things didn't look good, and she was having a hard time breathing. It's hard to describe the fear that overwhelms you when you hear the doctors telling you that your daughter might not make it. You feel helpless, but I knew we had to get everyone praying for her. Our parents called our extended family, and they filled the waiting room, praying for our newborn baby girl.

They let me go into the NICU to see her. I walked through the door, and there she was in an incubator with an oxygen tube taped to her face and monitors stuck all over her. I just prayed and sang to her. I brought a video camera in with me and then took it back to the recovery room so Jenn could see her. Those first few days were a blur of hoping and praying and crying.

Her numbers went up and down. Our family came in and prayed for her over the next few days, and they let Jenn in to see her. On the third day they even let us hold her. We stayed with my grandparents, who lived right by the hospital. They constantly prayed with us, and it meant a lot to have them be there.

Slowly Haley got better, and the doctors were amazed at her turn-around. She was in the NICU for ten days. It had been the scariest thing in our life. It was traumatic, but still it didn't send me into the kind of panic I'd experienced as a kid.

Once life normalized a bit, we continued working on our album. We were proud of the songs, and we couldn't help but be excited. We were actually making an album. After the initial recording sessions, I traveled to Andrew's studio in Santa Cruz for post-production, and we worked there for over six months to get the sound just right. I drove back and forth, and on one of those last trips to Santa Cruz, just when we were almost finished, all the audio files disappeared without warning. Hundreds of files vanished in a second, and the producer couldn't find them anywhere on the computer. We'd lost hundreds of hours of work. It was a nightmare.

The producer couldn't take it, and in the stress of the moment, he walked out of the studio. He needed to take a walk on the beach, he said. As I stood in the studio, I considered the consequences. If we didn't find the files, we'd have to start over and re-record. It was not an option, so I called Andrew and told him the bad news. He said his son, Joel Taylor, was in town, and if anyone could fix it, Joel could. He gave me the number, and I made the call to Joel. He came to the studio, sat at the computer and start-ed searching for the files. And one by one, Joel found the tracks and began piecing the album back together, like putting a puzzle together. It took two days, but he found everything that was lost and manually reconstructed the whole album.

Months later, the album released, and we started taking it on the road with us. We sold them at conferences and worship events. There wasn't any great fanfare surrounding the album, but it was well received by those who bought it, and we began hearing amazing testimonies on how the music was impacting people.

A couple of years passed, and I was writing more and more. Some of those songs began to spread beyond Bethel. But in that season, a well-known worship leader visited the church and said if I was going to write "the big songs," I'd need to write better lyrics. And though that sort of criticism would normally hurt, it was exactly what I needed to hear. I knew he was right. I wasn't a master songwriter, and I needed to improve. So, I made a decision: if the songs I was writing weren't good enough, I'd start co-writing with people who'd had successful songwriting careers. I knew I was good at coming up with melodies, but words were harder. I worked hard, and the songs got better. Written in community, the songs were stronger, and the process made me better.

Leading a team, Haley's birth, and the process of recording an album brought so much excitement but also pressure. I didn't realize it in the moment, though, because good things were happening. God was moving, and I didn't have the first hint of panic or fear. And so, without even realizing it, I did what I'd done as a child: I stuffed any pain and moved ahead to the next good thing God was doing. I didn't know more pressures were coming and would eventually land me on the couch, unable to cope with the basic things of life.

How can you know these things in your twenties?

NINE

THE COST OF FREEDOM

* * *

When we first moved to Bethel, it was a moderately sized church in a re-
mote county in northern California. Redding wasn't a destination in those
days. In fact, it'd never been a destination. Originally nicknamed "Poverty
Flats" by a priest who settled there during the gold rush, Redding wasn't the
kind of town many people wanted to live in; it was the kind of town people
drove through on their way to somewhere else. And though Bethel was a nice
church in the mid-nineties, it didn't have any influence or national recogni-
tion. But after only a few years, the church was becoming known as a place
where God was moving and miracles were happening. People from around
the world were visiting the church, and more and more people were attend-
ing our school of ministry.

My dad has always been the most humble, non-controlling, non-ma-
nipulative leader I know, and it was no different back in those days. He valued
a culture of freedom, and he wanted a leadership team that wasn't afraid to take
risks. He wanted a team with the courage to follow what God had put on their
hearts, and it was that same culture of freedom that created an atmosphere where
people could encounter God. As Bethel began to experience the benefits of this
kind of leadership, even more people came to be part of what was happening.

Many stayed and became a part of our church, and in just a few short years, our church doubled in size. With that growth our church staff doubled too.

The growth of the church staff brought its own challenges. We had good people with good intentions. People are naturally attracted to a culture of freedom because they want to be who God is calling them to be without being suppressed or controlled by a person or an organization. We weren't afraid of big personalities or people becoming big in our environment.

My dad wasn't interested in being a one-man show. There was room for a lot of people to be raised up and bring their voice to the table. As people step into this type of environment, it often can get messy. When people are on this journey and become big in God, they are bound to push up against some boundaries and make some messes. There is a price to this kind of leadership, but the fruit is evident. In the long run, it's worth it.

I could see the wisdom to this approach to leadership. It created an atmosphere that allowed our leaders to maximize their gifts and talents, but it wasn't perfect. We had a few leaders who had their own agendas, something that probably wouldn't have happened in a more controlling environment. And there was naturally more conflict, a thing that I usually avoided. What I didn't understand in those days was that conflict done well could have allowed me to understand where someone else was coming from and could have allowed them to hear my heart and perspective. But because I avoided it, a lot of things went unresolved, and I started to feel the pressure.

After a few years, we'd built a team whose musical talent and skill matched their anointing in worship. We pushed each other creatively, experimented and tried new things. I saw where God was taking us, and my eyes were fixed on the end game.

It seemed like every week lives were getting transformed. So many nights, we would minister to people after service. I remember one night a man was going through some emotional trauma, and I stayed there for hours quietly playing my guitar over him. I saw the freedom that came into his life just from simply playing a song from God's heart. That night I played for four hours, and I loved it; I was energized by it. It was a privilege to help someone else find the freedom that I had found in worship as a kid. I took what we were doing so seriously. I know these were holy moments, and I wanted the team to take it seriously as well. I wanted them to give as much to it as I was.

We had a drummer on our youth worship team, and we brought him up to play on the main team. Chris Quilala was only thirteen years old, and it was clear that he was talented and anointed. In his first few rehearsals, he fought back nerves, and during one of those rehearsals, he got a little too excited and broke rhythm as he tried to play a complicated fill. I stopped the band, told him the drummer's job was to help the band keep time, and until he could keep a steady beat to a click-track for five minutes, he couldn't play fills. I didn't follow it up with any encouragement, and even though I meant it as constructive criticism, it must have stung. All these years later, Chris and I laugh about that comment. We laugh about the similar comments I made to him over the years, and even though some of those comments made him better, the truth was, he was only a kid, and I came down too hard on him. I knew that great leaders know how to encourage and build people up while helping them grow, but I didn't always put those truths into action.

Looking back, I see how blunt I was. Even though some of the people on the worship team were young or hurting or broken, I didn't see them that way. I saw them as leaders, and I treated leaders differently. I had higher standards for the people on the worship team. The truth is, I often expected them to have it together. And as I pushed them, as I tried to force them into roles they weren't ready for or were naturally gifted at, I grew impatient.

Some of our team were at different stages of their development. I wish I would have remembered that there were people on the other side of my words. I felt like I was giving them so much encouragement, but Jenn would often tell me that one positive comment every few weeks wasn't enough for most people. But in my drive to achieve the vision, I'd become unaware of how my lack of words impacted people.

Looking back, I wish I had shared the heart behind my vision, the *why*. But I felt like I'd communicated the *how* and assumed everyone got it. I know now that assumptions almost always get you into trouble.

———————————

Emotionally it was a lot, but as the worship pastors, Jenn and I needed to spend time meeting with the musicians and worship leaders. Most of them were typical artists who were comfortable sharing their feelings. They often felt so much and wanted to communicate everything going on in their internal world, which was a lot because true creatives are often more in touch with their feelings and feel things deeply. That's how God made them, and it's a beautiful thing, but I wasn't able to see it then. I didn't spend a lot of time talking and thinking about my feelings and what was going on in my internal world (something I'm still growing in), so if one of our team members wanted to share how they felt, I'd try to avoid it at all costs.

All those conversations drained me. I was still learning how to lead a group of extremely creative people. My patience often ran short with the over-processors on our team. I started avoiding them. I didn't know how to help people take responsibility for their own growth, and so I avoided the conversations even more. If someone managed to corner me and drag me into those kinds of conversations, I'd end it as quickly as I could, and as I walked away, I made a mental note—*in the future avoid that person.*

For the most part, the team just wanted to feel connected and known by me, and although I couldn't pastor them all personally, my tendency toward avoidance wasn't meeting their real need for connection. We had a team of talented, anointed and sometimes broken people who needed me to be present for them.

I knew something had to change. We weren't able to carry the full responsibility of the emotional needs of our growing team, and so Jenn and I decided to break our larger team into smaller groups. We thought it might help them feel more connected, that it might relieve some of the relational pressure and stress. We hired multiple people to pastor the worship team because we knew how important pastoral care was, and Jenn and I weren't capable of meeting all of their needs. It was a good idea, and it took some of the relational pressure off me. I knew I needed to focus on being a husband and a dad to my kids, who were all really young. I also needed to spend more time developing my songwriting and growing as a musician.

Though we still did life together and hung out with the team all the time, I didn't dive into relationship with the key people on the team who really needed it. The team pastors gave me the time to do these things, but that also allowed me to disconnect a little more from the team. I didn't invest in them as much as I needed to. And if one of the team members came to me to discuss that disconnection, if I felt accused of not being present, I'd put more distance between us. I had a hard time knowing the difference between someone who really needed help and someone who was trying to get me to enable their poor behavior and decisions, and so I avoided both.

As the church grew, so did the opportunities to lead worship, especially in outside ministries and events. God was moving powerfully, and people wanted more of God. And though our worship team was growing, there were more opportunities than people to cover them all. Bethel was beginning to be known, and our young group of worship leaders were receiving invitations to lead worship at churches all over the world. It was an exciting time, but the constant invitations threatened the stability of worship at our local church. And we knew that taking care of our home church was our top priority in ministry because you can't export something that you don't have at home. Jenn and I knew it was our job to create a platform for people, and we didn't want our leaders to be small, but we also knew we needed to help them grow into their callings. We wanted their anointing to match their character.

Growing up in the church world, I'd seen worship leaders and pastors expand their ministries too fast. They'd burned out in the busyness of it all. Some had left their local church just before their marriage, family and relationship with God fell apart, and that was the last thing we wanted. What's more, Jenn and I knew what it was like to balance travel and raising a family, and we'd made our fair share of mistakes along the way. We wanted them to be rooted in God and their character so that they could grow their families in a healthy way and be able to handle the opportunities. Some people were really anointed but had things they were working and growing in. We wanted them to be set up for success when they went out.

Jenn and I were clear with the team. We set parameters around the worship leaders' travel schedules so they'd be rooted in the local church. The commitment would allow them to stay connected to the people of the church, and they'd create a pace that was conducive to growing a family. But we didn't ask them to do anything we weren't willing to do. We did our best to model it; we had three kids by then and knew we needed to be present for them. So though we were receiving our own requests to lead worship outside of Bethel, we turned many opportunities down and sent the teams that we felt were ready to go in our place. Some of our younger leaders caught the vision. Some didn't. It caused tension as some of the team wanted to travel more and weren't getting the opportunities. There were those who were on the road more than they were home. We wanted people to run at a pace that they could maintain for years, but they weren't setting a sustainable pace, and eventually they'd burn out. To make matters worse, as they traveled more and more, we had difficulty covering our worship services and events, and it was putting too much pressure on the rest of the team.

The frustration built as I tried my best to reign in the busiest of our team. I told them we were trying to help them set a sustainable pace, but still some of them didn't listen. I called more meetings, got louder and louder, but I couldn't seem to get through. It started to feel like Jenn and I were in the position to be the bad cops. As this feeling set in, I began making assumptions about their motives, and it became the lens through which I viewed their actions. I didn't give them the benefit of the doubt, and it created more distance.

It was a complicated time. We were building an amazing worship community, and God was doing so much. But still, I was navigating the conflicts that came with a talented group of individuals with anointing, vision and freedom. As our influence grew, there were misunderstandings. It felt as if no one heard me until I got louder or made a huge deal about something. I had a growing problem, and I needed the church leadership to help enforce some of the boundaries I'd set. The church leaders were all busy with their own responsibilities, and so they didn't quite understand why Jenn and I were so concerned.

Balancing the needs of the worship team was a lot. But there were layers to what was going on and so many growing pains. I was learning to navigate relationships with the leadership team of our entire staff at Bethel.

Every week at Bethel, our staff gathers for an amazing time where we share testimonies about what is happening at church and around the world through the different ministries. My dad started the weekly two-hour staff meeting years ago when things at the church were pretty tough financially so that if we had hard decisions to make, we'd make it from a place of faith and trust. It is a part of our DNA, so much so, that we still do it all these years later.

In those days, though, I didn't share much during those meetings. I didn't want it to look like I was promoting myself or Jenn, especially since there's nothing I hate more than self-promotion hidden behind the appearance of promoting God. Besides, the worship ministry of Bethel was so much bigger than Jenn and me, and I didn't want to run the risk of making it look like I was taking credit for all of it. So, I didn't share much in those weekly meetings.

As a result, some of the other staff members thought I was detached. And by not sharing, I didn't give people the opportunity to catch the vision of what we were doing and where we were going as a worship community. If I had communicated where we were going and the impact we were seeing, it might have helped people catch the vision for what was happening.

During those days money was really tight and all the teams were trying to get what was needed to take their ministry to the next level. Bethel leadership was trying to balance the budget as the worship ministry was expanding.

Our needs were growing, and I found my budget requests competing with the budget requests from other ministries. It's the way budget meetings always are. We needed better equipment to continue to grow, and that equipment certainly wasn't cheap.

For months I'd been working for better equipment. My requests were usually denied or delayed. I'd watch how we were spending money and became frustrated even though that money was invested in other ministries that were making an impact on our church and community. Worship could open a door to people's hearts. I knew major movements had been birthed from a sound or a song that captured what God was doing in a specific moment. I felt frustrated that the team couldn't seem to see what we were trying to build. Or at least it felt like they couldn't see.

In 2008, we had about a thousand students in our school of ministry, and Bethel continued to grow. We were on the edge of an opportunity and decided to livestream our services on the Internet. It was a great idea, and we were excited. We imagined people from around the world joining us, and the possibilities seemed endless.

Even though we were excited, we all knew it was going to be more complicated than we thought. We didn't know what we didn't know but knew we were supposed to move forward. There were technical aspects that needed to be thought through because no one was doing livestreaming on such a large scale back in those days. There weren't any churches that could give us guidance, and the technology was changing at such a fast pace. We were trying to keep up so that we could create a powerful experience for people who'd be watching online.

We moved ahead with the plan and invested in the equipment and crews necessary to make it happen. We were moving at such a fast pace, we were bound to miss a couple of things. Two weeks before the launch, one of the leaders stopped by my office and asked if the worship team would be ready to go. You could imagine my response.

What? In two weeks? How were we launching in two weeks?

It was in no way intentional, but in that moment I felt set up to fail. I asked how we were going to handle the sound for the stream and if we had hired a streaming sound engineer. I'd watched hours of poor-quality streaming audio from amazing and world-renowned bands. I knew if the stream wasn't mixed well, if it wasn't engineered right, even the most amazing bands sounded terrible. Getting a livestream right was extremely difficult even when you had unlimited budgets. We'd worked years on fine-tuning every part of the worship. My fear was that all of that would now go right out the window.

He certainly felt my frustration. I shared my concerns, telling him that the worship team wanted to be proud of what was streamed. We couldn't risk delivering a worship experience that didn't inspire worship. People needed to feel like they were in the room with us. I finally said that if they wouldn't hire a sound engineer for the worship, they couldn't stream the worship. I walked out of the office, the bad cop again. As the week dragged on, I stood firm, though I felt all alone, and after days of debate, it was agreed we could hire a sound engineer.

In hindsight, there was a better way to approach that situation. What I was wanting to protect was healthy and good. It wasn't the *what* that I was trying to protect that was wrong. It was how I went about trying to protect it. Approaching all of these situations as battles was starting to wear me down.

TEN

THE CABIN

* * *

By 2010, the worship team had hit its stride. We were seeing a lot of growth in our worship community: songs were being written, the livestream was gaining momentum, and God was moving. But we were also navigating the conflicts and misunderstandings that can come in a freedom culture.

In the middle of this growth, Joel Taylor—my friend who'd saved the day by finding all those missing tracks years ago—moved to Redding, and he started spending more time with Jenn and me. He would come to the house in the evenings to hang out with our family, and we would talk a lot about our vision for worship. We wanted to create something that served the church and made a way for artists financially. Maybe it was time to start the music label we'd always dreamed about. We could record the songs coming out of Bethel and make a new model for a label that was connected to the church and was sustainable.

We spent hours together dreaming about the label and doing things that had never been done before. We wanted to take what we'd built here—our passion for spontaneous worship and excellence in music—and get it out there. But we didn't want to create a new kind of music label just for the sake of creating something new. We wanted it to be focused on ministry with honesty and integrity and also to be financially viable.

When you create something new and bring it to God, it should cost something. It should bring people into an authentic encounter with God. When people have an encounter with God, they are marked forever. And that's exactly what we wanted. We wanted to see people experience Him. We wanted a healthy, mature team that was walking in authority and character who served the local church and carried that as they traveled. We wanted to gather people together to actively pursue God.

Bethel was bursting at the seams with worship leaders, musicians and writers. We needed a new structure that could manage the new season, all God was doing and the people God was bringing. We needed a CEO, a businessman who understood the music industry, and though this wasn't my area of expertise, Joel agreed to be a consultant until we found the perfect match.

We started interviewing potential candidates, but no one quite seemed right. They were all capable, all knowledgeable, but were from outside of Bethel, and they didn't seem to capture the vision of what we were trying to build. We kept interviewing but couldn't find anyone who fit.

After months of interviews, I walked into the kitchen. Jenn was already there cooking breakfast, and I asked what she thought about Joel coming on board as the CEO of Bethel Music. She agreed without hesitation, and as I reached for the phone, it rang. It was Joel. On the other side of the phone, he said he'd had the craziest idea. What if he became the CEO of Bethel Music? I told him Jenn and I had just been talking about this, and I'd been reaching for the phone to call him right when he called. We all laughed, stunned that after months of interviews, we'd come to the same conclusion on the same morning. Only God. We were so excited, and it felt right.

We'd found our CEO. We had a vision. We had an incredible team. And just like that, Bethel Music was born. Turns out, though, it takes more than a CEO and a vision to start a business. It takes capital. So, Joel and I developed a business plan, and when we had everything together, we took it to the church leaders to ask if they'd front the startup money. We presented the plan, but the leadership wasn't so excited, and history had something to do with that.

Prior to starting Bethel Music, Jenn and I had produced an album called *Here Is Love*. We'd taken a loan out from the church to cover the production costs, and the recoup time had taken longer than the church expected. Because I wasn't the best communicator, I hadn't managed the expectations for paying back the loan, and the leadership team was nervous. With an album, there's always an investment, and it takes time to recoup those costs. The team felt it was too risky. What if it didn't pay off? They went round and round. They wanted to support us, but this was also a time of growth for the church and finances were tight with so many needs for the local church. They discussed the pros and cons, but in the end they denied our request.

Looking back, I can see things from their point of view. The truth is, they were right. It was risky. But I knew we were supposed to do this. We were already seeing the impact, so we needed to move fast. We regrouped and set out to find funding. We approached a reputable Christian music distributor that had passed on our music years before—and we showed them the business plan. The distributor listened to our music, saw an opportunity, and jumped on it. They agreed to distribute the album for us, and they gave us an advance on our earnings. It was the loan we needed, but it also put us in a tight financial spot because from the minute we signed the contract, we were spending our future earnings.

The doors of Bethel Music officially opened, and we got to work. We began meeting with ministry leaders at the church, including Kris Vallotton.

Though he knew Bethel wasn't able to front the loan to start the label, he was excited about the vision and the direction we were heading. He wanted to help make sure Bethel Music wasn't spending all the advance on salaries. Kris knew we'd need to reinvest our royalties back into the label. He wanted the church to serve as an incubator for Bethel Music, and he found some money to pay Joel and a bookkeeper a small salary. It wasn't much, he said, but it'd help us to reserve capital to invest in what we were creating. We accepted, grateful the church was supporting the vision.

Even with the money from the distributor and the help from the church, our budgets were next to nothing. We worked in a tiny office that we shared with our bookkeeper, an intern and Joel. We knew if just one album didn't do well, Bethel Music wouldn't make it, and so we were careful about every decision we made.

We began recording the songs we were writing together, and excitement in the worship team grew. We released *Be Lifted High*, our first compilation album with all original songs, and it did better than expected. Still, we had no idea what was possible.

———————————————————

Years before, I'd been leading worship at Bethel when a phrase came to me during a spontaneous moment of worship. During baptisms, I began singing a simple phrase as a declaration over the people—*His love never fails, it never gives up, it never runs out on me.* I sang it over and over, and it seemed to resonate with the crowd. It was one of those rare moments of worship, a moment when you know you're singing something with power; and after that night, I'd often come back to that phrase in worship. Every time I did, it really connected with people.

I'd always wanted to write a song around that phrase, and I gathered a small group of writers to do just that. I invited Jeremy Riddle and Christa Black-Gifford and within a few weeks we had the verses and chorus well under way. We worked the song for weeks, went back and forth, and over the course of several writing sessions, we finished it. As we played it the first time, we knew it was special. What was born in a moment of spontaneous worship had taken seven years to complete, but it'd been worth the wait.

We introduced the full version of the song to the church, and they responded to it just like they had to the chorus. As I led it, I was reminded of what Matt Redman always says: "If it starts in worship, it will usually work in worship."

Finishing "One Thing Remains" marked a significant moment for me. Writing in collaboration had been one of the original dreams behind starting Bethel Music. We'd hoped to bring together songwriters from different movements to write songs for the church. That dream—a dream that had been in me for years—was finally starting to play out. We were bringing these ideas together and proving the concepts, showing how a consistent pursuit of vision resulted in powerful expressions of worship. I began to open up more too, and shared the successes of Bethel Music with the leadership team at Bethel. As I did, they began to see the vision that we had.

We kept writing, and in 2012 we decided to try to capture our next album. Even though we didn't yet have most of the songs written, we decided to go for it. Without much more than an idea, we gathered the team together and started brainstorming. We all agreed; we wanted to capture that unique sound we'd been building with our worship community, an organic and raw sound. And as we wrote for the album, what emerged was an intimate acoustic-driven sound. It felt totally different, and as the song list started to come together, our excitement grew.

Within weeks, we gathered at the studio, ready to record. This felt like one big experiment, and let me tell you, trying to pull off a live recording isn't for the faint of heart. It was stressful, but it started coming together. Joel was the project manager for the recording and film project, and he only had two unpaid interns helping him. In the middle of the project, we ran out of money. It was a major undertaking, and the deadlines on the project felt insane. But even though it felt crazy stressful, we tried to create space for God to move, to interrupt us in the way we always wanted Him to do. There were times we changed songs on the fly, sometimes in the middle of the live recording. We did all this while still trying to protect the integrity of the sound. In the middle of the project, we discovered our producer wasn't capturing the sound we wanted, so Joel and I stepped in and reproduced most of the songs we'd already recorded. What had been stressful was now downright chaos.

During the recording of *The Loft Sessions*, I felt so much pressure to protect the vision of Bethel Music, to fight for the integrity of the music and to create space for the spontaneous moments that I knew would make the album special. At the same time, we were trying to keep the project on track and control costs. It was exciting and overwhelming at the same time, but I kept all that stress to myself. At least that's what I thought I was doing, but it was leaking out on the team, Jenn and the kids. When we finished recording, we came together to listen to the album, and we couldn't have been more excited. We'd captured what we had dreamed about, despite all the difficulties and strains. Still the pressure in my internal world was building.

We finished *The Loft Sessions* and released it in 2012, and it seemed to take on a life of its own. People loved the sound, and sales of the album were beyond our expectations. I'd recorded "One Thing Remains" on both our first and second albums, and it began to spread nationally. That's when Bethel Music turned a corner.

Kristian Stanfill called, asking to record "One Thing Remains" for Passion Music, and we were stoked. Months later, he released it, and it took off even more. I started hearing the song on the radio. My friends called and let me know they were singing it at church and at conferences around the world. Well-known worship leaders emailed me, saying they were leading it at major events and arenas. Testimonies started pouring in, and people from across the world emailed to tell us how the song had changed their lives—the ultimate reward for a songwriter. And as those testimonies came, I saw how God could connect to His people and make them feel loved through a simple song.

In 2013, "One Thing Remains" was nominated for Song of the Year at the forty-fourth annual GMA Dove Awards—the industry awards for Christian music—and Jenn and I were invited by Shelly Giglio along with Kristian Stanfill to play the song live at the show. It was a surreal experience, leading worship for some of Christian music's biggest names. It was a significant moment, and Jenn and I could only feel overwhelmed by the faithfulness of God in that moment. God had given me the chorus in spontaneous worship, and co-writers had helped it fully come to life. And as I considered all the things that came together to make that moment possible, I felt nothing but deep gratitude.

"One Thing Remains" continued to grow in popularity, and it created a bridge for Bethel Music. It brought new opportunities to connect and collaborate with other songwriters, other worship movements and denominations. Worship leaders who'd written great songs for the church that I'd sung for years called to congratulate me and ask if I'd be willing to co-write with them. So many of these songwriters were personal heroes of mine. Things were going so well, and maybe that was why I ignored the building pressure.

There was a lot of crossover between my work with Bethel Music and the church, but balancing it all became more and more challenging even though I knew we were building what we were supposed to be building. We'd received so many prophetic words in the years leading up to Bethel Music, words that should have prepared me for the growing pains of being a young leader in a powerful environment. But I didn't realize that when you're creating something new, there's going to be some resistance, and people aren't always going to catch the vision of going to places that we've never been. I thought things were supposed to happen a certain way, and when they didn't, I became impatient. I didn't let those prophetic words give me the patience I needed.

We were devoting more time to the label, balancing our responsibilities at Bethel Church with requests to travel and lead worship, and preparing for our annual worship school. We needed a break from the weight of it all. Jenn and I decided to go have dinner with friends at a cabin up in the mountains. We were between Redding and the mountains when the text messages started flooding in. Some of the key artists and musicians from our team who were scheduled to help with the worship school had been booked by other church ministries. And all of a sudden, there I was in the same conversation I'd had so many times before. The frustration set in, and immediately I was livid.

Are you kidding me?

We told them that they had already committed, and we would have to scramble to fill their slots with other people who weren't as qualified. I was in the same conversation I'd had so many times before.

We pulled into the cabin, and I told Jenn how disrespected I felt. Wasn't this the same conversation we'd had so many times before? After what felt like years of fighting this issue, why were we still fighting over the same thing?

I talked it out with Jenn, at least she understood.

I immediately started texting my dad about the situation, but through the text exchange, it became clear we weren't seeing eye to eye. My world felt like a "free for all." It felt like things were happening to me, not with me. I felt misunderstood, a too familiar emotion. Without thinking, in the middle of our text thread, I typed words to my dad that had to sting.

I don't trust you.

I hit send, then looked at those words again. My dad was the best man I knew, so where had this come from? I was feeling so much hurt and pain that I hadn't even realized was there. It felt childish, and as I read that text over and over, I became more and more annoyed with myself. I was doing the very thing to him that I hated having people do to me—pouring out my emotional mess and expecting him to shoulder the load.

How could I be hurt by someone who would never try to hurt me?

And even though I knew it wasn't true, I felt hurt and angry. I was done trying to make this work or make sense. I didn't know how to win. Those words must have been a dagger to my dad, because he immediately texted me and asked me where I was. He said he was headed my way and was bringing my mom.

In no time, they were there, and I exploded with my bottled-up emotions, some I didn't know were inside of me. He wasn't anxious about any of it, and he didn't let it put distance between us. He listened patiently as I shared the frustration, the feeling of being misunderstood, the pressures, the lack of boundaries, the pain. I even talked about my vision and excitement for Bethel Music. It was all unfiltered and raw. The good emotions and the hard emotions—I didn't hold anything back.

Of course, I hadn't communicated how much this was affecting me before that night at the cabin. He hadn't understood the places I needed help. He apologized and shared how proud he was of me and of what we had accomplished. He could see what we were trying to build and was grateful for it.

As he shared, I felt really understood for the first time in years. I was tired and in pain, and my dad met me there. Some things would have to change, but talking with my parents had given me what I needed—the courage to keep moving ahead.

Although I was relieved after that conversation, I knew there were other conversations I had to have. I wasn't a great communicator, and I knew I needed to do better with our team. So, Jenn and I spoke with a father in our lives, Ray Hughes, who has taught at our worship school for many years. I don't remember a lot of the conversation, but at some point, he said to me, "Son, you're not great on your feet with words. Your emotions get the best of you. You need to write a letter. Write out what you need to say and read it." So, Jenn and I took time over the weekend to pray and write the letter, and in it, I wrote what I'd been feeling and what the next season needed to look like.

I hated every part of writing that letter. But my lack of communication about what we were called to do and how we were going to do it had been a mistake. I wanted God to be my defender and had thought He would step in; but in this season, it was my responsibility to clearly communicate what I felt like we were called to lead.

The letter was open and raw, which is where I was at that point. I could have worded things better, but I needed to set a clear course. Some of what I shared was intense, but I was able to communicate the vision for the future and the boundaries we'd need to accomplish it. It created some uncomfortable moments, but we were able to start a conversation and move through it. That was the first step in maintaining the relationships Jenn and I had for years with people we loved and truly believed we were called to lead with.

That night at the cabin started a new season. I'd resolved to share what God was doing through Bethel Music, and I wouldn't be so reserved with the church leadership team. I'd begin investing more in relationships, and I'd try not to make assumptions when I was frustrated. I'd share more about where we were headed as a worship community. It required some hard conversations, but things did get better.

But when the pressure seems to lessen, you can trick yourself into thinking that your internal world is doing well. I couldn't have put words to it back then, but the truth was, I'd spent too many years burying my feelings in an attempt to manage the pressure and stress. I didn't know that feelings buried alive never die. I assumed that if I wasn't feeling any frustration or hurt in the moment, then I must be fine. I didn't realize that there were unresolved areas that I wasn't aware of. New opportunities would come, and as things continued to grow, those areas would be compounded by new challenges that we would be facing.

Some people say time heals all wounds. I know now that time just lets wounds fester.

ELEVEN

CLEARING BLACKBERRY BUSHES

* * *

It felt like a new start. We started developing more leaders and musicians. And things were better now that we had healthier boundaries in place. But there were patterns that I'd established for years, habits and automatic responses that didn't disappear overnight.

As our schedules became more demanding, things became hectic, busy and noisy. With the increased pace of life, Jenn and I needed a peaceful place, a retreat for us and our kids. So, though we loved our house, we started looking for a large piece of property where we could have a little farm.

For months, Jenn stuck to a routine. She buckled Braden into the car seat during his afternoon nap and looked at properties while he slept. She searched Redding and the surrounding area, and during one of those afternoon drives, she finally stumbled upon it. She called me at the office and told me she'd found an incredible place east of town.

"Babe, the property is incredible! The trees are amazing. It's like a secret garden," she said. "It's twenty acres, and it needs some work." There was a rundown house on the property, but she thought that with some renovations it could be just what we'd been looking for.

I dropped what I was doing, jumped in my truck, and headed out to see the house. I pulled down the driveway, and Jenn was waiting for me with Braden on her hip, smiling. I climbed out of the truck, and we started to explore the property.

The property was overgrown with blackberry bushes, vines and brush. The house was completely rundown, but the land was beautiful, and it had so much potential. Everywhere I looked, I could see deer and wild turkeys, and I was stoked. I got excited as I considered the possibility that I could hunt on my own property. There was nothing I loved more than watching deer and hunting.

And best of all, it was only a couple of miles from the church. Jenn and I had always wanted a small farm, and as we looked around the property, we knew it was perfect. We'd always dreamed of having a home where we could have community nights for our worship team as well as hosting friends from around the world. We knew that was part of what we were made to do. I could see it all, our community, a little farm with animals, and plenty of space for my kids to run and play. This was our dream piece of land, and we knew it right away. We had to have it.

I asked a contractor to come out and take a look, and we walked through the house. We talked through a remodel and building an addition. It would take some time, he said, but it was doable. I left the meeting, went home, and talked to Jenn. It seemed like a no-brainer. We were going for it.

The next day, I told our family and friends that we were going to put an offer on the property, and I invited them out to take a look. They followed Jenn and me out to the land, walked the property, and took a look at the house. They could see the potential of what we wanted to build, but they also shared their concerns. "The place is so rundown, and the property is so overgrown," they said.

I knew it'd take a lot of work, but I could see what it would become. It was a special place. I pushed off their concerns, deciding this would be the place we'd build our dream home. The following week, we went to the bank and started the loan process. Though it took over nine months to clear escrow, we finally closed on the property.

Within days of closing, the contractor began work. Three months passed, and then six. Progress was slow, and the house remodel was well behind schedule and already overbudget. New invoices kept rolling in even though I couldn't quite tell what they'd done. My frustration was growing.

During the endless construction phase, Jenn came home from leading worship at a conference in England. She walked through the door, told me to sit on the couch, and launched into the story of a powerful experience she'd had after one of the worship sessions. A woman had approached Jenn and asked if she could pray for her. Jenn agreed, thinking it'd be a quick prayer, but instead, this stranger led her in a two-hour inner-healing session.

She started by telling Jenn, "I feel like the Lord wants to talk to you about the past seven years of your life." That's exactly how long we had been managing some of the hard things in ministry. Jenn felt the Holy Spirit and knew He was about to speak to her. She then had Jenn ask the Holy Spirit, "What lies have I been believing?" Instantly the Lord spoke to her, "You've believed you haven't loved well, that you haven't led well, because if you did, no one would leave you." Jenn started bawling as this woman and the Holy Spirit showed her it wasn't true. She didn't even realize that she had believed that, but it made sense and had felt true.

As they prayed, the woman spoke directly to particular situations she couldn't have known about, and she led Jenn to examine the areas where she'd been holding onto unforgiveness, unforgiveness she didn't even know was there. She helped Jenn see how she sometimes responded out of pain and how that pain had influenced some of her relationships. Jenn repented and let people go in her heart. Afterward, Jenn felt like fifty pounds of weight had fallen off her and realized that she'd been carrying around so much extra baggage that she wasn't even aware of.

During the prayer, the woman spoke to Jenn about me. She asked about our new house—a detail Jenn hadn't told her—and said that she felt like it was a metaphor for my inner life. Jenn asked me to call her as soon as possible because she hoped it would be as impactful to me as it had been for her. "It might be insightful," she said.

A couple of days passed, and though I wasn't really excited about the idea, I agreed. After only one ring, a woman with a British accent answered the phone. She began telling me about her time with Jenn. She knew all about the house, but she wanted to hear more about it from me. She asked how the property was connected to what was going on in my life, and I told her I wasn't sure.

She kept pressing, asking me to describe it, and I said vines were growing inside the house because it hadn't been lived in for over two years. The land was overgrown with poison oak and blackberry bushes, and I mentioned how trying to clear those vines and bushes from the property had been a full-time job. But even with all of that, it was a special place. And though others couldn't see it, we knew we could turn it into something beautiful.

She asked about my life, and I shared about some of the internal struggles that had only just come to light. She circled back to the property and said she felt like it was a metaphor for what was happening in my life with the land overgrown with brush, poison oak, blackberry bushes, briars and vines. She prayed over the internal struggles and encouraged me to personally be part of dealing with the overgrown land. She felt like it was a prophetic act that would mirror the process that God was going to do in my heart.

The next morning I hired a small crew. We started pulling out the poison oak, and after a few weeks of work, we moved on to the blackberry bushes. We created what seemed like thousands of burn piles on the property, and the work was slow going, but after a year, the land was starting to shape up. There was something about clearing those vines and bushes that felt therapeutic. And soon I'd be dealing with the overgrown vines of my internal world.

Our property was a full-on construction site. It was a lot of change, and we had left a beautiful house to live in the middle of it all. One morning as we were making breakfast in the kitchen with the kids, we couldn't even hear ourselves talk due to the massive saw cutting through the sheetrock of the kitchen wall. In the beginning we could laugh it off, and we had good days and bad ones living in the mess of it all. But four years passed, and still the house wasn't finished. Contractors and workers were all over our property and in our house, and the permitting process was a nightmare. The remodel dragged on, and we were paying way more than originally expected. I'd been given time frames and budgets, but it seemed like those were just nice ideas. The pressure built, and every interaction started to feel like a nightmare. So much of the house was half-completed, and as I'd inspect the work, my frustration continued to grow. We didn't have clear communication of where we were in the project, when we could expect it to be completed, or what the final cost would be. It felt as if I were trapped, but I didn't know what to do.

We had no idea what was normal with construction, and so, near the end of one of the remodel phases, I called my friend Jason, who is an experienced builder, and asked if he'd help me manage the project. He agreed and drove to the property. He had a strong conversation with the contractor—not another nail could be hammered until Jason examined the property.

Jason called me as he walked through the house. Things weren't lining up, he said. We needed a new contract, and I asked if he'd take care of it. He agreed. A few days passed, and Jason delivered the contract to the contractor. We'd need a schedule for completion, proof that the contractor was making efforts to receive permits, and a firm budget. By the time he left the meeting, the contractor had signed the contract and agreed to the conditions. Things were back on track, but the pressure of living in a construction zone for over four years had definitely taken its toll.

It wasn't just the work stress and the stress with the home remodel. I'd also hired a financial manager, and things weren't going well. When we spoke, he seemed to overcomplicate everything, and he was always apologizing for not delivering on essential filings. There were so many balls being dropped, and it made me really nervous. Unsure of what to do, I hired another financial advisor and asked him to review my records and give me an assessment of where I was.

It took a few days to get through the records, and it soon became apparent that things weren't being handled as they should be, and there were potential major problems. I asked what I should do, and he suggested that I get my books in order.

I fired off a very clear email to my soon-to-be ex-financial manager, telling him I was terminating the relationship. By the end of the day, my files were transferred to a new firm, and even though a crisis had been averted, even though I had someone I could trust in my corner now, the pressure still built. It was a perfect storm, and to make matters more complicated, the issues with the house and my financial manager had all come to a head on the exact same day. I felt like I was about to pop.

——————————————

Even in the middle of the personal chaos, the team at Bethel Music was stretching creatively, and excitement was growing. We began working on a new album, *Tides*, hoping to continue the acoustic sound we'd developed in *The Loft Sessions*. But as we worked the songs, the music took a turn. In production, we found ourselves pushing the envelope with the sound, and since it was a studio album, we took some musical risks we weren't able to take in a live setting. The experimentation as always put us behind schedule.

It was a risk we were willing to take, but I still wasn't completely pleased with the sound. The producers were doing an incredible job, but I knew that we could make it just a little bit better. There is a fine line between excellence and perfection, and I often moved back and forth across that line. I wanted them to make it excellent, but the standard created intense pressure for the entire team. And though I loved the sound that resulted from the drive for excellence, it still came at a cost.

——————————————

We released *Tides* and went out on tour with the team. Our cash flow was better, but money was still really tight. We'd met with the bigger touring companies but realized we couldn't afford them. We were also told multiple times that in order to be successful in touring, we would have to be on the road four to six weeks at a time. There had to be a better, healthier way to tour and take care of our families.

So, we started an internal tour and events team, and as we always seemed to do, we got really scrappy to get things off the ground. Joel wore multiple hats and was our stage manager, oversaw volunteers, booked flights, and handled lighting. I was the band leader and worked with our sound engineer to dial everything in. Everyone pitched in, loading and unloading the trucks and working the merch table. It was exciting but exhausting.

We had friends in the music industry and saw firsthand how the demand to be on the road was affecting families and marriages. We were doing our best to protect family, so we made sure that our artists could bring at least some of their family on tour without incurring extra expense.

And as we traveled together, we grew so much closer as a team. Nothing draws people together like sharing life on a bus twenty-four-seven. As we traveled, an amazing thing started happening. I was able to get to know our team of artists and musicians better. We connected, and I was able to really see what made them come alive. I would have avoided this type of connection in the past, thinking it would be too demanding. But as we traveled, I realized all that relational time didn't drain me like it used to. In fact, it gave me energy, and in that, I learned to love our bus tours with the team and how it bonded us together even more.

The touring, the success with the music, came with its own set of pressures. As the label, distribution, income, and expenses grew, each decision became more and more important. We wanted to leave space for where we felt God was leading us, wanted to reinvest in the right places, but there were so many needs within the label. What had once felt like a small mom-and-pop shop was becoming a well-organized machine.

In the early days of Bethel Music, we were more laid back and able to go with the flow. We did most things relationally, and our agreements were verbal. But as the ship grew bigger, we realized we needed to tighten up our processes. We needed to make hard decisions about the music we produced, and we needed to formalize our relationships with contracts so that we were all on the same page and all had the same expectations. We learned some hard lessons and made mistakes, but we were growing and learning.

We built a music publishing company and formed inhouse design, marketing and engineering teams. Our own internal touring team was managing multiple events around the world, sometimes simultaneously, and we were building our own recording studio. Add to that, we were responsible for the worship of the church, including our growing worship school and our online worship school. I wasn't just busy. Amazing things were happening, but I was spread too thin.

I'd always been most excited about songwriting and leading worship, but now that I was part of running a label, I was more and more involved in the nuts and bolts of the business. Each month it felt as if I was stepping into a new role on any given day.

As my responsibilities grew, it became harder and harder for me to do the very thing I was so passionate about—write worship songs. I constantly adjusted my schedule and made time to write. Writing kept me energized and excited, and the songs were coming with more frequency. I did my best to keep collaborating with other artists, and in my spare moments—whether at a stoplight, in line at the coffee shop, or at a break in a business meeting—I'd text an idea to a co-writer. Whether I was writing with someone from our team or a friend from another worship movement, I'd almost always end up writing the bridge. It's funny looking back now, but all I really wanted was to be a bridge in the worship community and that was often the role I was playing in songwriting.

In those days, I kept my iPhone on the music stand whenever I led worship. I found that most of my good song ideas came when we were in worship, and I wanted to be able to record them in the moment. If a spontaneous moment hit, if I knew there was something on it, I'd step away from the mic, grab my iPhone, and hum the melody into it so I wouldn't lose it. Then I'd step back to the mic and continue to lead worship. This was how the song "Forever" began.

During a spontaneous moment on a Sunday morning, I got a melody, and I sang it into my iPhone. Later that day I played it for Joel. I ran all my ideas by him because he seemed to know when a song had staying power. He loved it, said there was something to it, and suggested writing around it.

A year later, Kari Jobe (now Kari Carnes) came to co-write with Jenn and me. We worked on two songs, one of which was "Forever." I sang the chorus, then started to step out of the room when I heard her humming a melody that stopped me in my tracks. I asked her to sing it again and recorded it on my phone. I knew when I heard it—that was the melody for the verse.

We didn't finish the song while Kari was here but continued to work on it over the next few months. The song was almost ready, and we went to the studio to record it. There was a minor problem, though. We hadn't written all the lyrics yet. We hoped we'd find the missing lyrics, and while in the studio, one of the producers had an idea for the opening verse: "the moon and stars they wept." It felt like it came out of left field, but we tried the line. There was just something about it that strangely worked, and we knew we'd found the missing lyric. It was just what the song needed. We recorded "Forever" just minutes after we'd finished it, and it was well named because it had taken forever to write.

The following Sunday, I lead the song with Jenn at church, and as we got to the end of the song, Jenn began singing spontaneously and unrehearsed.

We sing alleluia
We sing alleluia
We sing alleluia
The lamb has overcome.

She sang it over and over, and we all sensed the power of the moment. And even though we thought it was finished, it became clear that this would fully complete the song. Right after the service I called the producers and told them to scrap the recording. We needed to record it again with the new bridge.

Months later we were recording another live album, *You Make Me Brave*, and Kari was set to lead one of the songs on the album. But before sound check, Kari and I changed plans and decided to have her try singing "Forever" instead. In the middle of her singing the song for the first time, she broke down in tears. We listened as she sang with such raw emotion and authority, and it became obvious in that moment. This was her song.

When she sang "Forever" during the live recording, it was only the second time she sang it. "Forever" was a song that was birthed in worship, finished in worship, and recorded in worship. Even though it was such a long process, this was the way I loved for songs to come to life. God was a part of the entire process, and I never quite knew how it was going to unfold.

As Bethel Music expanded, we kept our eyes open for artists we felt God was highlighting. So many of our artists were discovered in our worship school, but some came through our touring and events. But as much as I loved finding new artists, what kept me going was the writing, the creating, the collaboration. I was always on the lookout for people who carried that carried the same heart that we did, people like Jonathan and Melissa Helser.

While on tour, Jenn and I connected with Jonathan and Melissa. We'd listened to their album and it was emotional, raw, unfiltered, and you could just feel God all over it. One night, they joined us backstage, where we talked for what seemed like hours. We fell in love with them, and I asked them if they'd fly out to Redding and explore co-writing. Weeks later, the four of us sat at our kitchen table discussing the impact a song could have on the church. They wanted the same thing we wanted, to raise up a community of worshipers and to change the world through songs. As I listened to their vision, I told them the church needed what they carried, which was a raw, passionate approach to worship. People needed to hear their music.

We had started working on another compilation album, *We Will Not Be Shaken*. It was a project we'd wanted to record live on top of a mountain overlooking Redding. We wanted the album to capture our community, similar to what we had done with *The Loft Sessions*. But when we told the production team where we wanted to record, they told us it was going to be way more work than we expected, and it would be difficult to capture on top of a mountain. There were alot of unknowns. It was a crazy idea, but we also knew it'd be amazing if we could pull it off. So we decided to go for it.

We were still selecting songs for the album when the Helsers sent us a couple of unfinished songs. One was a demo that had a half-written verse and a powerful chorus: "I'm no longer a slave to fear. I am a child of God." I heard it and knew they had to record this song for the album. But like "Forever," it wasn't finished.

I sat with the song for a few hours, and I found a melody for the bridge. I sent it over to the Helsers, and we started kicking around ideas for the lyrics. We worked the song right up to the last minute, just like we did with so many songs. It was coming down to the wire, but twenty minutes before the recording, we finished it. We walked in and recorded it, and you could feel the power on the song. From the beginning, we knew it had something special on it. It really connected with people and carried so much transformation.

Those were good days even if they were full and complicated. I was balancing so many things—the highs of writing and producing new songs, the pressure of building a ministry, the changing team dynamics, our house remodel, raising a family, managing situations that we didn't have answers for, leading a team of over one hundred worship team members, and figuring out my role in the middle of it all. But as long as I was still writing, I wasn't able to see the effects of the strain and pressure. I always thought that once I got through the next thing, the pressure would ease up. But next things never stopped coming. Victories don't relieve the pressure. The joy I got from my family didn't fix unresolved issues. Pressure catches up with you, and if you don't deal with it, eventually you'll pop.

TWELVE

THE DRIVE HOME

* * *

We were well into fall, months after my breakdown started, and still each day was an ongoing battle. I cut everything I hadn't already cut, but the panic was still there with me, just below the surface. I needed my anxiety medication just to make it through each day, and while it held me together, it also brought the numbness.

Jenn was exhausted picking up my slack. She did everything for the kids in those months. She woke them up, fed them, got them to school, disciplined them, put them to bed at night, and everything in between. But she wasn't just covering for me at home. She was covering for me at the office, too. She attended all the meetings, met with Joel to help make decisions about the label, traveled for the ministry, and led the worship team. I was amazed at how strong she was, but still she was worn thin, and at the end of every night, she fell into bed, exhausted.

One afternoon, she fell to the floor and just started sobbing to God that she couldn't do this anymore. She heard Him give her the verse Lamentations 3:28: "When life gets heavy and hard to take, go off by yourself. Enter the silence. Bow in prayer. Don't ask questions: Wait for hope to appear. Don't run from trouble. Take it full-face. The worst is never the worst." She held onto that as a lifeline; it was going to be okay. But she was running on empty and needed a break. More than anything, we needed a break together. We needed to reconnect.

Jenn came to me and said, "Let's go to Napa for a few days. Maybe getting away will be good for you, good for both of us."

It was a great idea. Napa was our retreat, the place we went to unwind. It was only three hours from Redding, and with the great food and beauty, it was one of our absolute favorites. Maybe it would be good for us to get away and reconnect, I thought. Getting away from my routine might give me some small measure of relief. But even as I considered the trip, I wondered if I could make it without having a panic attack. I remembered the hunting trip to Pennsylvania just a couple of weeks before. I'd thought that trip would be good for me, but I never imagined how it would go.

Weeks before Jenn suggested a trip to Napa, I traveled east with my friend Sean Feucht and my father-in-law, Ron, on a hunting trip for whitetail deer. We'd planned the trip well before my breakdown started, and though things had changed, I didn't want to miss it. I wanted to do something that felt normal, something I loved that might help get my mind off the panic of the past few months.

The three of us packed our bows and made our way to the airport. In the car we talked and kept it light. But as I walked to the plane steps, I could feel the fear start to increase around me. I tried to shake it off and was determined to carry on like nothing was happening.

But as I walked down the aisle and made my way to my seat, those unwelcome but familiar feelings of panic were right there with me. I turned to Ron, making small talk with him in the hopes of avoiding the inevitable, but nothing changed. A few minutes passed, but I hadn't heard a word he said. I tried my best to hide it, but it was no use. Ron knew what was happening in my life, knew the level of panic I was wrestling with, so I finally told him I was really struggling. I apologized, reached into my bag, and grabbed two pills. I knew this wasn't going to end well without help. I swallowed them dry, sat back in the seat, and closed my eyes.

I made it through both flights pretty sedated. By the time we finally got to Pennsylvania, I was discouraged. This season wasn't letting up, and I wondered whether it would rob me of everything, even the joy I got from hunting.

I slept through the entire night, and I woke early the next morning, excited for the first day of hunting. It was one of the few normal things that I'd done in months, and I'd decided the panic and anxiety weren't going to ruin it. I was going to enjoy it, no matter what. And for a while I did.

On that first day, while sitting in the treestand, I felt more like myself than I had in months. It was a small glimpse of hope. The second day was like the first; I felt almost normal. But as I sat in the tree stand on the last evening of the trip, and the sun began to set, exhaustion set in. And this was not the normal kind of tired you sometimes feel at the end of a long day. It was a deep exhaustion, the kind of exhaustion that's more than physical. I dragged myself back to the lodge, and as I did, the exhaustion grew. When I finally saw the lodge just over the hill, my mind started playing games with me. I could feel the unsettledness that often came before the anxiety and panic set in.

I walked through the front door, went straight to my room, and called Jenn, hoping a conversation with her could settle my nerves. I tried to make small talk, asking how her day had gone. She could hear it in the sound of my voice though and knew something was off. "Are you okay, babe?" she asked. I tried to compose myself, tried to keep from crying, but it was no use. Through tears, I told her it felt like I was coming apart again.

The worship team was at the house for a meeting, Jenn said, and she'd ask them to start praying. I found out later that the team came together and prayed for me for hours. Most of the team prayed for me at their houses through the night. The power of a praying community should never be underestimated.

I told her I loved her, hung up the phone, and turned toward the door. Ron and Sean were standing there, waiting. They'd heard me sobbing, knew something was wrong, and they'd come to my room. "The panic has set in," I said, and I couldn't breathe. And as soon as I said the words, I fell into a full blown meltdown. I knelt at the edge of the footboard and started shaking. I buried my head in my arms, broke out in a cold sweat, and closed my eyes, trying to will the panic away. It was another big one. I was falling apart and knew I needed medical attention.

"I need to go to the hospital," I told them. "Please."

"The closest hospital is over an hour away. I feel like we're supposed to get through this without the doctors. We're going to get through this together," Ron said. He spoke with authority and put his hands on my shoulders and prayed while Sean grabbed his guitar and began playing and singing worship music over me. I'd like to say the anxiety left the minute they began playing, but it didn't. In fact, it ramped up. And as my breath drew shorter and my heart pounded harder, I begged even more for them to take me to the hospital. Still, they wouldn't.

They went after it with more intensity in prayer and worship while I knelt there on the floor. I squeezed my eyes shut even tighter and searched for the first sign of relief, and after what seemed like fifteen minutes, the panic started to ease. It was still there, heavy on my chest, but I became more aware of Ron's prayers and Sean's worship. They'd never stopped. They stood with me through it all. I was more than grateful to them both.

My body was no longer shaking, and I finally lifted my head out of my arms. Peace settled over me. I looked at Ron and Sean and thanked them for helping me avoid another trip to the hospital and sticking with me. I climbed into bed, and within minutes I was asleep.

The next morning, as we packed up to head home, we started talking about how intense last night had been.

"Bro, last night was crazy," Sean said.

I told Sean again how grateful I was. "It was a moment when worship was the only thing that could break through the torment and bring relief."

Sean agreed, but then he said, "Yeah, but it sure lasted longer than a moment."

"I don't understand," I said. "My panic attack was only about fifteen minutes."

He smiled and shook his head.

"Nah, bro," he said. "I played over you until three in the morning, until you finally fell asleep."

I had been lost in the panic for hours? How had Ron and Sean stayed up with me that entire time? They'd carried me through one of the darkest nights and into the morning, just like my dad had so many times so many years ago.

We flew back to Redding, and when I arrived back at my house, I walked the property. The construction crews were everywhere and the normal sounds of our kids were instantly too much for me. The attack had been an eye-opener, and I saw it—the medicine wasn't healing me; it couldn't heal me. Things weren't getting better, and I didn't see an end in sight. Hopelessness fell on me like a blanket. I understood how someone might see no other option but to turn to drugs or alcohol or anything to numb their pain. I saw how living in such chaos and torment might lead someone to believe they were out of options, how it might lead someone to take his own life.

In that quiet moment, under all that weight, I was more convinced than ever that God was my only option, and I was going to get through this.

I knew that God would pull me through this season. I didn't know how, but something had to change.

———————————————

Just two weeks after the hunting trip, Jenn and I decided to head to Napa. It was a good idea, I told her, even if I had some apprehension. We packed our bags and dropped the kids with their grandparents for the weekend. It would be two days alone together in our favorite place with amazing food.

We had a great drive down, and it was so nice to just be together. We pulled up to one of our favorite hotels and stepped out of the car. It was a familiar place where we always came to decompress and spend time together. But even as I walked in the hotel, I could feel the pressure, and that's when I knew it—there'd be no peace on this trip.

We spent the first evening at one of our favorite restaurants. I tried to ignore everything and have a normal meal, but it was no use. I did my best to relax, to keep everything light, but I couldn't stop the chaos of my mind and emotions. I fought to get a grip, to just make it from one moment to the next. But after struggling through dinner, Jenn leaned across the table, took my hand, and said, "Let's get out of here."

We went back to the hotel and tried to watch a movie, but the anxiety was too much. Sleep didn't come in the hotel room that night, and I ended up pacing the floor till morning. Jenn stayed up with me, told me she could feel the anxiety in the room. She prayed over me and reassured me I was okay and that I would get through this. Each time I woke up in the night, she got up with me and didn't fall asleep until after I had. She later told me she'd experienced my panic in a whole new way. And as heavy as it was on our first night in Napa, the second night was no different.

By the morning of our second day, the sleeplessness had taken a toll on both of us. We were exhausted, slow-moving and groggy—we both knew I wouldn't find the peace we had hoped for. We decided to cut the trip short and head home. We packed our bags, loaded the car, and set off for Redding.

We were both disappointed and frustrated with how the trip had gone. It was not the getaway we had planned to reconnect. We were silent through the first part of the drive. Neither of us wanted to say out loud the hopelessness we were both feeling. We had tried everything, and nothing was changing. I was trapped in myself, desperate for answers, and in that moment it felt like it was getting worse.

Jenn broke the silence first. She said she hadn't realized how bad my anxiety could be in the night, and I told her that was because I tried not to wake her when it hit. She was already carrying so much of the responsibility, and I didn't want to bother her with one more thing in the night. Being in that small hotel room had given her a sense of how bad it really was.

My thoughts felt heavy as we drove in silence for a few more minutes. Jenn turned back to conversation. She began asking me about things that had caused me pain in the past. We'd talked through times I'd been hurt before, and I'd thought I'd fully processed the frustrations and the emotions. I believe in inner healing and was sure I had dealt with any areas of unforgiveness. But this moment was different. I'd been pushed into a corner, and it finally allowed me to see my past in a new light.

I wasn't feeling the Lord but still could sense that this was a significant moment. There was a grace that came on Jenn, and she led me through some deep inner healing. She had me ask the Holy Spirit to bring to mind a name of someone I needed to forgive. As soon as she asked the question, names started coming, and I spoke them out loud. Some of the names were obvious, names I would have expected because they were people I'd had conflicts with in the past. Others were names I would have never thought of, names attached to what seemed like petty offenses, but I realized I needed to forgive them.

Jenn kept pressing, and as she did, she led prayers and asked me to repeat after her. She led me to confess unresolved conflict, unseen grudges, and hidden bitterness in my heart. I finally saw the pain that I didn't know was there, and as I did, I could see there was still forgiveness that needed to happen. There were situations that I could now see with such clarity—places I never knew I'd been hurt, and I needed to let them go.

As I began to confess this bitterness, as I spoke the names out loud, I saw my own part in some of the messes. I'd made small choices, done things that had seemed inconsequential at the time. I'd failed to communicate or had avoided conflict altogether. I began to see how much these things mattered. The things I'd swept under the rug were amplified and highlighted as we prayed, and I could see how God was showing me just how important they were to Him.

I'd thought ignoring the feelings was the best option but now could see it brought me to a breakdown. Those actions had affected my relationship with others, with myself, and with God, and now God was leading me to make it right.

Jenn asked me about random and obscure thoughts she had, the people and situations of my past, and then asked how that word would make me feel. Each time it would have meaning and we would follow where that seemingly random thought took us. It was always significant and powerful and led to a place where I understood just how much forgiveness was needed.

The bitterness and unforgiveness were nothing more than sin, and I needed to repent for it. If I was going to make it to the other side of this breakdown, I couldn't hold onto any form of unforgiveness. I confessed it all and resolved to live a different way; and in that commitment, I felt a real sense of hope. It felt like my soul was clean. God had used this experience to prepare my heart to encounter Him in a whole new way.

As the anxiety decreased, I felt a new freedom. We kept talking for the remainder of the drive, and the mood in the car grew lighter. God had come to me in my darkest hour of need, and a new peace was taking hold. I wasn't sure how I'd maintain this peace, but I was overcome with the sense that I needed to give myself to the Word of God.

As we pulled into the house, I knew that the Lord wanted my devotional life to change in a major way. There was a deep knowing that this would be crucial to my healing. I resolved to fully give this next season to God and myself to the Word. Even as I made the commitment, I knew it would be the key to not just getting well but staying well. I was going to surrender my life in a way that I hadn't up to this point, and it would make all the difference.

As I walked into the house with Jenn, I knew something had changed. The anxiety was still there, but it was not nearly as strong. And though I felt like the panic could come back, the sense of hopelessness had disappeared. I had new clarity. I'd found the light at the end of the tunnel. There was a knowing in that moment. The war had been won even though the battle was still being fought.

I took a deep breath, deeper than I had in months. I looked at Jenn and started crying. She was crying, too. We both knew it—we were going to win.

Everything changed on that drive back from Napa. I'd always known the value of spending time with God and that time in His Word was important, but God had made it clear: His Word would restore me and renew my mind. It wasn't just a good idea or principle anymore. It was the missing link, the thing I needed for healing, and the only option that would bring stability to my life.

In my desperation, I came to the point where nothing worked—not medication, not less work, not hunting trips, and not time with Jenn. I had no option other than to fully surrender to God, and He'd met me when I was at my darkest point. He kept me from falling back into that pit and sinking even further away. I came to realize this truth: consider it a gift when God becomes our only option.

THIRTEEN

THE DAILY SURRENDER

* * *

That drive home gave me new courage and conviction to press into my pain. Even though I knew God hadn't given me the panic, I realized that He wanted to do something through it. How did it all work? I couldn't say, and I couldn't work out the tension and mystery in all of it either. But I knew God was doing something, and I wasn't going to fight against it anymore. I wasn't going to try to numb my panic. I was going to let go, surrender, and trust where God was leading me.

I had new hope, and that night I made a plan. I set my alarm for 5:15 a.m. the next morning. I slept hard that night and when the alarm woke me, I was ready to go. I got up and made my way to my leather chair. I had recently been given the Passion translation of the Bible, and I decided to use this version. I wanted to start with a new copy that had unmarked pages to bring a fresh perspective.

As I turned the pages, I wondered which chapters and verses I should read first that morning. Even as I started, I sensed God reminding me that my devotional life was going to look different than it had before, and I didn't need to worry about getting through a certain number of verses or chapters. There was no goal but spending time with Him, no agenda other than connection.

I was going to slow everything way down. I wasn't in a race, and I needed to let each word get into my spirit. I turned to the book of John and started taking in each word really slowly. As I was reading, the words leapt off the page, and I knew there was a grace for this season. I felt a closeness to God. He was near, and this was the direction I was supposed to take. I was completely content to fall into this season of peaceful connection and pursuit. It was unexplainable, but I knew I was on the right track.

I wasn't trying to get anything, and it wasn't about accomplishing something. In those moments, I had no desire to try to accomplish anything. It felt like it was just God and me, and I was experiencing what it would be like in heaven. I'm such a goal-driven person that my devotional time had become more about quantity time rather than quality time. But now there was a carefree way that I could approach time with God.

I meditated on the words, and I stayed in that chair until the kids came into the kitchen just a couple of hours later. I walked to the espresso machine to make Jenn a coffee. When she came into the kitchen, I told her about what I had experienced, and I could see she was as hopeful as I was.

I didn't have anything to do that day, so I mostly worked around the house. I took it easy, and as I went, I kept my mind fixed on the words God had given me. Once the kids were asleep I got into bed that night, and I realized that I'd made it through a day without worrying once about falling into a panic attack. And though I couldn't say the threat of anxiety wasn't present, the panic hadn't won. I could quote the scripture about renewing your mind through the Word, but in these moments I was really experiencing it. Finally the panic didn't have the edge, and it was such a personal victory for me.

The alarm woke me at 5:15 a.m. the next morning, and I got out of bed excited to see where God would take me. I felt His nearness. I opened my Bible, and again the words leapt off the page. God was giving me exactly

what I needed for the day as I meditated on the verses and let them get into
me. I knew God was telling me that this was exactly what this season was all
about. I was in the will of God, and I felt a peace that was so powerful even
with the presence of the panic. Peace in the panic is hard to imagine, but it
was there, and the ability to surrender to the will of God is so simple when
you're experiencing that peace.

I was learning what surender truly meant on a new level. As the
day continued on, I thought about the coming year and could feel the Lord
reminding me to stay present in the moment. He was asking me not to
think about the next year, the next month, or even the next day. He'd given
me enough grace only for today. I sat in that truth, and I could feel the
peace that came to me when I focused on fully living in the moment I
was in.

Morning after morning, I had the same experience. I'd sit in my leather chair and pick up where I had left off the previous day and start reading. It
was a surreal experience. God was giving me the words I needed for the day
that would unfold. And with those words came an unexplainable grace and
peace. The Word was alive. God was preparing me to be fully successful each
day through my devotional time. It didn't matter where I had stopped reading
the previous day; what I was reading each morning was exactly what I needed
for the coming day. And as I lay in bed each night, I could look back and see
just how faithful God had been.

I reflected on the years I'd lived from the big prophetic words about
my life that spoke to the upcoming months and years ahead. But as I experienced this new kind of daily living, I could see how weeks, months and years
of victorious living started first through daily receiving. God was reminding
me of the truth in the Lord's Prayer—give us this day our *daily* bread. I realized that so often I want weekly, monthly or yearly bread. But living only for
the future had robbed me of the grace to live each day well.

As the week continued on, I stayed with the same rhythm, and each morning, God took me to the exact places in the Word that I needed for that day. It was different each time. Sometimes it was a verse; sometimes it was a theme; sometimes it was just a feeling. It wasn't about doing it a certain way, a formula. It was about the consistent, daily investment in time and relationship.

For the first time in months I knew I was winning and beating the anxiety. I had a clarity of mind I hadn't felt in months. And though I was still taking the anxiety medication, I didn't want it to be part of my life anymore, and I wasn't afraid to explore what it would take to get off the medication. I didn't want to need it anymore.

At the end of the first week, I scheduled a doctor's appointment, and by the following week, I was sitting in her office. I told her how I'd had a breakthrough, and I wanted to get off the medication as soon as possible. She listened, and when I finished telling her about my Napa experience, she let me know, "You've had a mental breakdown, and up until now, you haven't been giving your mind what it needs to heal itself. It sounds like God has stepped in and done something. But still, you're going to need to take it slow."

She reviewed my meds and dosage. "What you're taking is a benzodiazepine," she said, "a drug prescribed to those suffering from anxiety disorders, severe panic and irrational phobias. It's given to calm nerves before surgery, to keep patients from resisting general anesthesia. It's a drug tailor-made to hold off a meltdown. But like any other benzodiazepine, it's also a drug known to lead to physical dependence, abuse and addiction. It's one of the more potent benzodiazepines, and people who take it regularly can develop increasing tolerance to it. With that increased tolerance often comes an increase in dosage, mostly self-prescribed."

That completely described my experience. The longer I'd taken it, the more I had to take in order to knock back the panic. She paused, let me wrap my mind around all that information, then continued.

She told me it'd be hard, but I could do it. I couldn't quit cold turkey, or else there'd be a risk of withdrawal symptoms. If I didn't do it right, the panic attacks might come back stronger than ever. I had to take my time.

I agreed, and she walked me through a plan to start to taper the meds. She prescribed something new, something less addictive that would help keep the anxiety away as I weaned off my medication. I took the prescription and the plan, and I walked out of the office hopeful.

I began cutting my meds slowly. I could still feel the effects of the medicine, but something had changed. The panic wasn't waiting for me around every corner, and my world wasn't closing in on me anymore.

Kris Vallotton came to see me. He shared how he'd overcome his own breakdown almost a decade ago. He'd read a book, and it'd been a great help. He handed me a copy of *Panic to Power*, by Lucinda Bassett, and I thanked him and told him I'd read it.

It wasn't a self-help book written by someone trying to convince you to overcome your panic with only joy or gratitude. Instead, it walked through the scientific realities of a panic attack, what actually happens when the anxiety comes and a person feels out of control. Bassett shared how panic is actually your brain's way of trying to protect the body from long-term damage. It was a way of stilling the body so emotions could catch up. As I read, I began to understand. I wasn't broken. In fact, my body was doing exactly what it was supposed to do. It was trying to send me a message.

I just needed to listen to my body, slow down, and allow God to set my pace just like He'd been doing in my morning devotionals. And that realization brought so much comfort. What God had spoken to me—slow down because I've only given you the grace you need for today—had been confirmed by science. God knew exactly what my body needed, and He'd given me information to confirm it.

I was sitting in my living room watching TV that evening when the terror began to creep in. I wanted to run to the kitchen and grab a pill to numb the panic. But I knew that instead I needed to lean into the fear.

I laid down in the middle of the living room with my arms and legs outstretched, and I closed my eyes. It was the most vulnerable thing I could think to do. It was the thing I feared the most in that moment, being so exposed. I felt the panic start to close in, and everything in me wanted to grab another pill and make it stop. I recognized that anxiety for what it was, though, my body's defense mechanism, and I knew it was trying to send me a message.

Slow down. Don't run. Listen.

It was a significant moment, a moment for God to do what only He can do. Even as the panic rolled over me in waves and threatened to sink me, I stayed on the floor. I kept telling myself the panic would end, my body couldn't keep producing these panic-inducing chemicals forever. I reminded myself that God would see me through this, and that's what He did. When I thought I couldn't take any more, I felt Him reaching in, steadying me, bringing His peace. After only a few minutes, the panic passed, and I was at peace. It was a victory I needed, one that came only when I settled into the moment with God. I was on the road to recovery.

I'd kept my nervous breakdown relatively quiet. I had shared with some close friends, but now I felt like it was time to share what was happening in my life with the worship team and the staff on the label. At our next community night with our worship team, I shared what had been happening over the last few months. I was pretty emotional and cried my way through the meeting. It felt so vulnerable and raw as I shared how scary and powerful it is to be in a place where God becomes your only option. I asked for their prayers as I continued to heal. I knew bringing in community was crucial at this point. Jenn and I both wanted the strength of their prayers to give us strength through this season.

That moment of vulnerability was a milestone for our entire team. We were able to reconnect with why we were doing what we were doing: the Presence of God. We'd been doing good things and growing as a team; there had been so much momentum. But it's easy to get a bit lost in the busyness when you see such good things coming from your ministry. We were going to recalibrate to make the main thing the main thing.

A few weeks passed, and per the doctor's orders, I cut my dose by another quarter. I made it through the next days without incident. I didn't have any panic or anxiety attacks. In fact, I felt freer than I had in a long time. I finally was able to really connect with Jenn and the kids. We had a great time over the holidays, and it was amazing to feel fully present again with everyone.

My energy was higher than it'd been before my breakdown. The small imperfections or normal things that would have set me off didn't bother me anymore. By the end of just a couple of months, I was off of all anxiety medicine. It felt like God was carrying me, and I knew my mind was healing. I went to see my doctor, and she shared how incredible it was that I was able to get off the anxiety medication so quickly.

Even though I was off the medication, I needed to keep pushing into the Word. Every day was a new experience of grace. Every day brought an increase in peace, clarity and hope. I understood the truth in Philippians 4:12: "Christ's explosive power infuses me to conquer every difficulty."

With a clear mind, I could now see how the meds had been nothing more than a crutch. It had helped me along at first, and I wouldn't have been able to get a grip without it, but over time I'd come to rely on it to numb the panic and pain. I used it to ignore the underlying wounds. Then that moment of clarity came on the trip back from Napa, and I could see that I'd treated the symptoms of panic instead of getting to the root cause of the panic.

So many of us use crutches to avoid our pain: drugs or alcohol or food or porn. We might use money or status. Sometimes we even use good things in the wrong way, like sports, relationships, careers or hobbies. We continue to numb ourselves, ignoring all that pain, but if that pain goes untreated, it becomes infected. It's that kind of infection that poisons us from the inside out. And no one is exempt from this kind of poisoning.

There are times when all of us need a crutch. There are times when medication can give you a foothold or at least a temporary relief from the panic. But crutches are designed for seasons. Eventually, you have to throw those crutches out and learn to walk without them. I was learning to feel the pain and work through it with God, to deal with the real root of the matter. God wanted to bring complete healing and wholeness to my life. He wanted to fully restore me.

For me, the path to wholeness started with pulling out the roots of bitterness and unforgiveness on the ride from Napa. That drive gave me the moment of clarity I desperately needed so that I could see that a change to my devotional life was the crucial next step. But I knew that conversation with Jenn and confession to God weren't the only steps I needed to take.

As God healed my mind through the Word, it became clear to me that there were tough conversations that I now needed to have and was ready to have. Jenn and I scheduled meetings with those we felt there were still unresolved issues with. Before each one, I would get nervous, but the panic never came. I cried my way through most of those meetings but was able to be vulnerable. There was mutual understanding, and we were able to restore key relationships.

We committed to a new way of doing relationships going forward. I wouldn't withdraw when I felt misunderstood. I'd deal with things in the moment and talk about how I felt. They committed to the same thing. I wanted to have whole and healthy relationships. I needed that for my own peace of mind.

As we mended those relational breaks, we began to experience this truth: forgiveness is rarely a silent thing. In order to experience the full power of forgiveness, the pains of the past have to be talked about and dealt with. Reconciliation has to be pursued, explored and chased after.

Hindsight is perfect, and in hindsight, I can see that none of us had bad motives. None of us were out to hurt each other. We were all doing the best we could. We loved each other. Still do. It was just that sometimes our pain and issues got in the way. If I'd been more honest with myself, if I'd been more vulnerable with my pain, years of misunderstanding might have been avoided.

But maybe avoiding the pain isn't the point. God works through breakdowns—I know that firsthand. He used mine to bring me to the end of myself. I was falling more in love with God and people every day. I was experiencing the ultimate revelation—God is faithful to the end.

———————————————

Everything changed in the months following the drive home from Napa. What had once been the most painful season of my life gave way to something beautiful and filled with hope. And though God didn't curse me with those months of debilitating panic, He did work through it.

How does God work through pain? How does He use it? I didn't understand it back then, and to be honest, I'm still not sure I understand now. But I've come to see that none of my own efforts to ease the pain, pressure and tension worked. It was my full surrender to the process with Him that brought peace.

Pain is never God's endgame. He allowed it to bring me to the end of myself. Brian Simmons says, "The heart that remains innocent will progressively see more and more of God." That's exactly what God had done—He'd restored my heart so I could see more of Him.

———————————————

Months after my last attack, I walked from the bedroom and into the kitchen. The kids were at the table, eating breakfast, and Jenn was standing at the sink. She looked over at me smiling and said, "Brian, you're singing!"

"Yeah?" I responded, wondering why she had said that.

She laughed. "I've always been able to tell how well you're doing by whether you're singing around the house or not," she said. "Outside of worship, I haven't heard you singing for months."

I thought about it. She'd used music to gauge how I was doing, something I'd never thought to do. But as I considered it, as I thought it through, I knew she was right. I was in a good place. I was at peace.

FOURTEEN

WHEN GOD BECOMES REAL

* * *

I stood near the stage between Braden and Jenn, worshiping. The invisible hand that had squeezed my lungs at the river was gone. The weight that pressed down, the panic that drove me to the hospital, had disappeared. The pressure I'd carried for so many years was gone too.

Everything felt limitless, and I could feel God with me. I hadn't missed a morning spending time with God. He daily gave me what I needed through His Word, and there I received the grace I needed for each day.

I hadn't let things build up in the months of my recovery, either. As the stresses, pains and pressures of life came, I took time to recognize it and first bring it to God. Sometimes I just needed to work it out with God. But then there were the times that I'd need to talk through the issues with friends, staff members or even Jenn, and we'd work it out. I'd learned it was important to deal with issues quickly before they had a chance to grow and become a place of disconnection.

In the same way, if someone confronted me with an issue, I'd listen, and if I had caused it, I'd do my best to clean it up and own my part. Through the practices of daily time in God's Word, walking in forgiveness, and confessing my own failings and faults, I'd found peace.

I hadn't written anything in months, but as my mind and spirit continued to heal, the songs started to come again. There was a new grace for writing and melodies started to come out of nowhere. It was work, but it never felt hard. There was so much life in these songs that carried hope and promise, songs that matched the season I was in. I found myself feeling more alive as I began collaborating with my friends. I was writing from the reality of what God had pulled me through. I knew I was made to write worship songs for the church. I wanted others to get to experience the grace and breakthrough I had found.

I hadn't yet shared my journey publicly though many at Bethel knew something was happening in my life. Still I hadn't yet communicated the details and severity of what I had gone through. But a few weeks before, my dad had asked if I'd share my story. And I knew it was time. As I walked to the stool in the center of the stage, I didn't feel an ounce of anxiety or nerves. I honestly felt carefree in the grace of God.

I knew the power of my testimony.

God had healed me.

I scanned the crowd. I looked to my right, saw Braden next to Jenn, and smiled. He waved. "Hey, bud," I said, waving back.

Braden had been right by my side in my darkest hour. He'd ridden shotgun with me through one of the worst panic attacks, even though he didn't know it. Dang, I love that boy. Pride overwhelmed me as I thought about how the kids had watched as I struggled but never lost hope. And now here they were, listening to me share my story. I remembered the moment when it had all started, the moment I'd looked them in the eyes and told them, *This is when God becomes real.* They'd been part of one of my lowest moments, and now, after months of barely surviving, they were witnessing the victory God had brought me. This was a family victory and had become part of our history with God.

I looked at the crowd and launched into my story. I told the whole story. I'd been a stress case, I told them, a guy who didn't look at his feelings or admit to the pain of life. I'd ignored conflict and the complexities of everything. I'd tried to pretend it couldn't affect me and just pushed through. But in all of that, unforgiveness had taken root.

"Our culture often teaches us to man-up," I said, "instead of admitting that we're hurting or feeling any pain. We were designed to feel the pain and then bring it to the Father. That's what Jesus did. He felt the pain and laid it at the Father's feet."

I pulled a red balloon from my pocket, stretched it three times.

"This balloon is like your heart. And as hurtful and stressful things happen to you, a pressure builds."

I blew into the balloon.

"We weren't made to hold on to and carry that pressure. We're made to take it to God and surrender those things to Him."

I took the balloon and filled it up, stretching it to capacity. "So many of us try to avoid the stress and pain of life, try to numb it, or pretend like it's not really affecting us." I looked at everyone. "And then one day this happens." I popped the balloon with a pen.

"And that's what happened to me," I said. "After years of internally holding onto stress and pain, my life popped."

I told how the stress and strain had built. "Some people turn crazy not because they want to," I said, "but because they can't bear the weight. They weren't supposed to. That's what happened to me. No one can bear the weight of unforgiveness and stress alone. No one."

I talked about the coping mechanisms I'd created over the years, how I could ignore the pain and conflict and just work harder. I tried to protect myself from pain by distancing myself from people or whatever caused me stress. But those coping mechanisms never worked. In fact, they only increased the pressure.

"There will come a time when you can't avoid the stress of life or numb the pain anymore. And when your coping mechanisms don't work anymore, consider it a gift. Consider it a gift when God becomes your only option."

I made my way through the rest of my notes and encouraged people to come clean with the things they used to try to numb their pain. "Experience the pain," I said, "and bring it to God. You'll find Him faithful."

———————————————

After the service, Jenn took the kids home, but I stayed late to talk with people. They told me how the message had helped them and asked for prayer. As I drove home that night, I realized sharing my story was the last step in my healing process. All those revelations about forgiveness, pain and pressure had come through months of daily time with God and having the hard conversations that were necessary.

I turned down the road toward my house and thought about the days when I couldn't even leave because everything was too overwhelming. And though I could still remember the pressure, though some days brought stress, I'd learned how to press into God, and then the chaos didn't have power in my life. I'd learned to communicate better. I'd learned how to stay grounded in His Word. The uncontrollable panic was completely gone. It was a daily process, and I was gaining more and more history with God on how I wanted to live my life.

I thought about the people at church that night. They needed to hear someone say, "I struggle too." We are all desperate to know that we aren't alone and are looking for a glimpse of hope. If there was anything God had given me over the last few months, it was hope.

Turning down the driveway, I saw the lights coming through the windows. I walked through the door, and as I did, Braden ran to me and wrapped me in the biggest hug. I hugged him back, grateful, looking forward to our next hunt for lizards.

The pressure was gone, the panic a memory. There was nothing but peace. It'd taken what seemed like an eternity to get here, but I wouldn't trade it for the world. That season of darkness had opened my eyes to the reality of a better way. That darkness gave way to light. It was in that darkness God proved Himself faithful. It was in that darkness when God became real.

WHEN GOD BECOMES REAL

_____

FOR MORE INFORMATION:

WHENGODBECOMESREALBOOK.COM

BETHEL MUSIC

BETHEL MUSIC IS A COMMUNITY OF WORSHIPERS PURSUING THE PRESENCE OF GOD.

WE EXIST TO GATHER, INSPIRE, AND ENCOURAGE THE GLOBAL CHURCH TOWARD DEEPER INTIMACY WITH THE FATHER.

TOGETHER, WE EXPRESS WHO GOD IS AND WHO WE ARE IN HIM, CAPTURING FRESH EXPRESSIONS OF WORSHIP IN EVERY SEASON.

BETHELMUSIC.COM